The Forgotten Resting Place

The Forgotten Resting Place

Copyright 2018 Lisa Buffaloe (updated July 2023)
John 15:11 Publications, Florence, AL 35630

All rights reserved. No part of this book may be reproduced or transmitted in any way, form or by any means, electronic or mechanical—including photocopying, recording, or by any information storage and retrieval system— except brief quotations in printed reviews. without permission of the author.

Visit the author's website at https://lisabuffaloe.com

ISBN-13: 978-0692132401
ISBN-10: 0692132406

Cover photo and design: Lisa Buffaloe
Photos: Lisa Buffaloe

Printed in the United States of America

The Forgotten Resting Place

Contents

Looking for a resting place 1

Session One 5
    Resting in perfect love 7
    Resting in The Father 14
    Resting in fellowship 19
    Resting in grace 28

Session Two 39
    Come aside and rest 40
    Resting in forgiveness 45
    The Rest of forgiveness 54
    Beyond the scars 64

Session Three 74
    Head rest 75
    Overwhelming 89
    Resting in trials 96
    Resting in the wait 106

Session Four 115
    Storm stability 116
    God's calming, comforting hope 123
    Resting need 133
    Circumstantial rest 142

Session Five 149
    Resting equipped 150
    Power praise refreshing 160
    Resting in the power of prayer 166
    Moving on rest 173

Appendix: Information about Jesus and Heaven 183
About the Author 188
Books by Lisa Buffaloe 188
Acknowledgements 189
Bible credits 190

Footnotes and Scripture 192

The Forgotten Resting Place

The Forgotten Resting Place

Looking for a resting place

Bad news, people angry and hurting, politicians battling and belittling, the media's agenda leaning right or left, overwhelming life difficulties, and the world seems to have gone stark-raving crazy. I don't know about you, but I need a safe place, a place where I can take a deep breath.

I read this verse and could so identify, "**My people have been lost sheep. ... They have wandered** around in the mountains. **They have roamed** from one mountain and hill to another. **They have forgotten their resting place**" (Jeremiah 50:6 NET Bible).

There are many days I feel like a little sheep wandering and roaming in search of a resting place.

And then, my heart moaned when I read this verse in Genesis ... Noah, "sent out a dove from him, to see if the water was abated from the face of the land; but **the dove found no resting place** for the sole of her foot, **so she returned to him** into the ark, for the water was on the surface of all the earth. Then **he put out his hand and took her and brought her into the ark to himself**" (Genesis 8:8-9 NASB).

I can visualize the little dove without a place to rest her feet, and the gentleness of Noah's touch as he returned the dove back into the ark, back into his presence. In the same way, our tender, loving heavenly Father longs to bring you into the safety and rest of His presence.

There are moments, days, weeks, perhaps years, you have been searching for a resting place.

Immanuel, God with us, holds out nail-scarred hands and says to the one needing rest, to the one so restless, "**Come to Me, all who are weary and heavily burdened ...,** and **I will give you rest [refreshing your souls** ... for I am gentle and humble in heart, and **you will find rest (renewal, blessed quiet) for your souls**" (Matthew 11:28-29 AMP).

Just as the dove needed a safe place to rest her feet, our souls also need rest. I wish I could bless you (and me) with a quick two-step process to finding a resting place. Unfortunately, I can't. As a matter of fact, as I write this study I'm in one of the most painful battles I've ever faced. The Lord knows I need a resting place.

You too may be in the midst of a battle and hardships. Various problems, concerns, and worries hit us all. It's a tough world out there.

God beckons, "**Rise up, my love, my fair one, and come away**" (Song of Solomon 2:10 NKJV).

Rest isn't the absence of problems, rest comes as you spend time with The Timeless One. Heart rest comes with the One who made your heart. The One who loves with an unfailing love wants you to know you are loved.

Know and breathe deep of The Life who gave you life.

God and His truth lead to our resting place. "Be still and know that I am God" (Psalm 46:10). Being still and knowing God is an invitation, a discovery, an offer of fellowship with our loving Creator. The One who created you, longs to spend time with you.

Jesus told His disciples, "Come aside by yourselves to a deserted place and rest a while" (Mark 6:31 NKJV).

The God of eternity beckons our hearts to come aside, rest, to be still and know that He is God. "For I have given rest to the weary and joy to the sorrowing" (Jeremiah 31:25 NLT).

Like the Psalmist wrote in Psalm 131:2, my prayer is that our souls will be "Like a baby content in its mother's arms, my soul is a baby content" (MSG version).

I don't have the answers, but God does, so we will search God's truth for His answers to find rest. As you go through this study, I'll be honest with you about my struggles and battles, and I promise to always point to God, His Word, hope, grace, comfort, healing, and encouragement.

Every reference to scripture will be made with the hope that you will linger slow and allow God's Holy Spirit to provide comfort, guidance, reassurance, and refreshing. God's word is where rest is found in this crazy restless world.

Although there are five sessions, please move at your own pace. At the back of the book, I've included each verse referenced so that you have the freedom to take the study wherever you may go.

For comfort and rest, please add your name into the following verses...

_____ has been a lost sheep and wandered and roamed from one mountain and hill to another. _____ has forgotten _____ resting place. _____ found no resting place so _____ returned to God and He put out his hand and took and brought _____ to Himself.

Jesus tenderly beckons, Come to Me, _____ who is weary and heavily burdened, and I will give rest, refreshing your soul, for I am gentle and humble in heart, and you will find rest, renewal, blessed quiet for your soul.

(Jeremiah 50:6 NET Bible, Genesis 8:8-9 NASB, Matthew 11:28-29 AMP)

Session One

Resting in perfect love

Greg Lucas related a story about his son, Jake[1]. Jake is an autistic man-child in his twenties with the cognitive abilities of a two-year old. Greg, his wife, and Jake attended church or attempted to attend church. They sat in the back so they could exit if needed and tried to keep Jake quiet. However, Jake zeroed in on the ending of the pastor's sermon. The pastor gently prodded his congregation to go beyond a hello or handshake to perhaps give a hug.

Jake took the pastor seriously. At the sound of the closing "Amen" and before Greg and his wife could stop him, Jake bolted and zeroed in on an older gentleman trying to leave before anyone caught him.

Jake didn't just hug the man, he bear-hugged him. Greg was horrified at the man's stiff body and angry frown. But then, he saw moisture in the man's eyes, which gave way to a softening body and face as he returned Jake's embrace.

Before Greg again could stop Jake, he broke free. Jake ran from person to person, almost bowling over people, hugging, laughing, squishing, and slobbering.

That precious young man opened rigid doors that had never been opened before.

God's love shines in the most unique out of the box places. His light beams on the special needs of us all. We're all broken, messy, needy children in need of The One who loves us through the broken, messy, neediness of our lives. Sometimes love is painful, slobbery, smushing, squishing but it's perfect love, and that love is available for you.

- **Read 1 John 4:15-18[2].** (Find the passage in your Bible or in the back of the book.) **Who is God? What casts out fear?**

God is perfect love, and He cares for you, perfectly loves you, and in His perfect love, fear is gone.

Let's get to know perfect love. This side of heaven, we can't fully fathom the depth and love of God. But I do know, God loves you. He really does. God's love is not like human love, there is no imperfection with God. God's love is pure, clean, and perfect.

The richness of human love can't compare to God. His love is beyond the gentlest touch, the sweetest kiss, and the warmest embrace. Imagine the most tender love ever known, and multiply it by infinity and perhaps, just perhaps, you have a small glimpse of God's love.

All the days were written in God's book before you were even born. God knows the number of your days and wants to be with you all of those days. He formed you in your mother's body, lovingly knitting you together (Psalm 139:13, 16).

Nothing is ordinary about how you were created. God made you extra-ordinary.

Consider, an average heart beats eighty beats-per-minute, which means your heart beats about 4,800 times per hour and 115,200 times per day. If you took all the blood vessels out of an average adult they would be close to 100,000 miles long. Truly, you are fearfully and wonderfully made (Psalm 139:14).

No one is like you, no one can replace you, and no one fills God's heart like you.

- **According to Psalm 139:17-18[3], how many times does God think about you?**

- **Psalm 121:1-4[4] and Zephaniah 3:17[5] share some wonderful insights about God. What does He do while you sleep?**

- **You are so special to God. According to Matthew 10:30[6], what does He know about you?**

- **Based on Isaiah 49:15-16[7], what assurance does God give and what has he done?**

God thinks constantly about you and rejoices and sings over you while you sleep. He is intimately acquainted with you. He knows the number of hairs on your head and your name is inscribed on the palms of His hands.

God loves with an everlasting love and with an unfailing love draws you to Himself (Jeremiah 31:3).

- **According to 1 Corinthians 13:4-8a[8] what is love?**

Since God is love, that means He, as love, is patient, kind, not envious, does not boast, and is not proud. God is not rude, is not self-seeking, is not easily angered, and through the grace of Jesus keeps no record of wrongs. God's love does not delight in evil but rejoices with the truth. He always protects, always trusts, always hopes, and always perseveres. God never fails.

Throughout the Bible are examples of God's love, how He pursues and woos, protects, and holds out His loving hands. To know more about God, we have to spend more time in His Word.

The Bible gives insight into who God is and the beauty of how much He loves His children. God's word brings wisdom, guidance, comfort, encouragement and help for every need.

What we know about God and what we believe about God makes an impact on our lives. If our relationship and belief on God is based on faulty information, we will act and react in the wrong manner.

What do you know about God?

Do you base your knowledge on what you see and experience, on what someone else tells you, on the circumstances of life, or on the Bible? What you know about God determines how you live. What you know about God determines your belief, trust, and actions.

- **Read Matthew 25:14-29[9].**

In the passage Jesus shares the story of a master who before leaving on a journey entrusted his property to his three servants. The first two servants took action on what was given to use and multiply the master's gifts.

The other servant dug a hole and hid the master's money. The Greek definition reveals the last servant "concealed" and "kept secret" what had been given by the master.

When the master returns, he settles accounts with his first two servants who were faithful to use and multiply what they were given.

- **Read the following passage. How does the master respond to the first two servants in Matthew 25:21 and Matthew 25:23?**

The third servant with the one talent responds, "Master, **I knew you to be a hard man**, reaping where you did not sow and gathering where you scattered no seed. And I was afraid and went away and hid your talent in the ground. See, you have what is yours" (emphasis added on scripture).

The servant's incorrect actions were based on his own incorrect knowledge. The master had freely given him a gift. However, instead of the servant using what was given, he concealed and kept secret his talent.

He buried what was given, then gave it back unused and unappreciated. As a result, what he had been given was taken away and punishment given. For most of my life, I looked at this passage as a warning to use the gifts given by God. I believe the warning is true, but I wonder if Jesus isn't trying to also make another point?

When assumptions are made and beliefs are based on one's own limited knowledge, the blessings of God and the fellowship with God are missed.

Knowing the love of God, knowing God is your loving Father who wants the absolute best for you, allows freedom to live in the abundant joy Jesus promises. Christ Jesus gifts with salvation, a gift to be appreciated, cherished, loved, and used for the glory of God to further God's kingdom.

God blesses with His presence, with His gifts, and with His salvation, truly we can live in the joy of our Master. The passage in Matthew 25 continues with Jesus sharing about the judgement and separation of those who were faithful and those who were not.

Please be sure you have taken and received the gift of salvation offered by Christ. Jesus offers the gifts of mercy and grace to all who will believe and receive. And, when the gift of salvation is received, the receiver becomes a conduit for Christ to work and bless others.

"Because if you acknowledge and confess with your lips that Jesus is Lord and, in your heart, believe (adhere to, trust in, and rely on the truth) that God raised Him from the dead, you will be saved. For with the heart a person believes (adheres to, trusts in, and relies on Christ) and so is justified (declared righteous, acceptable to God), and with the mouth he confesses (declares openly and speaks out freely his faith) and confirms [his]" (Romans 10:9-10 AMPC).

- **Have you given your life to Jesus Christ? If not, would you be willing to read the section titled "Questions about Jesus and heaven" toward the end of the book?**

Just as a loving father will take care of his children, God longs to take care of you. He longs to carry you close to His heart, love you and enjoy fellowship with you.

- **Read Isaiah 41:10[10], Isaiah 41:13[11], and Psalm 94:18[12]. What does God do and say?**

God's lovingkindness holds you, holds you up and tells you to not be afraid because He will help you. Jesus promises the eternal safety of God's hands. "I give eternal life to them, and they will never perish; and no one will snatch them out of My hand. My Father, who has given them to Me, is greater than all; and no one is able to snatch them out of the Father's hand" (John 10:28-29 NASB).

The enemy, no one, and nothing can snatch you out of the safety of your heavenly Father's love.

The picture given in Isaiah 40:11 shows God's tenderness. "He tends his flock like a shepherd: He gathers the lambs in his arms and carries them close to his heart; He gently leads those that have young" (Isaiah 40:11 NIV).

Truly, our God is a gentle, loving Father.

Resting in The Father

Perhaps you have a hard time picturing God as your father. Maybe your dad wasn't the best; perhaps he was distant, beat you or abused you. I'm so sorry if that is your story.

Psalm 68:5 tells us that God is a Father to the fatherless, and many may feel fatherless because of an imperfect father. Please know even if you didn't have a loving earthly father, you have a Father in heaven who loves you with an unfailing, perfect, and pure love.

I saw a wonderful example while I waited at an airport. A father arrived home, and his wife and two little girls ran to embrace him. The father hugged his wife and then hugged each little girl. He then bent down to look at each one individually and to listen to what they had to say, all the while his loving gaze remained captivated by his little girls.

That is who our God is -- a heavenly Father who leans down from heaven to tenderly cup your face in His hands and tell you how much He loves you and is so glad you are His.

In the Barcelona, Spain 1992 Olympics, Derek Redmond was touted as one of the best. His awards were many and included World Silver and Gold Medals in the 400m and 4 x 400m competitions.

Derek had trained and prepared for the 1992 Olympics. He knew the risks. As an athlete in the 1988 Olympics, an Achilles tendon injury forced him to withdraw only a few moments before the race.

Four years and five surgeries later, he was determined to medal in the 400. Barcelona would be his opportunity. No matter what, he would finish strong. During each qualifying race, Derek ran well, recording the fastest time of the first round and winning his quarter-final heat.

Jim Redmond, his father, watched in anticipation as Derek settled into the starting blocks for the semi-finals. Derek made a clean start and quickly took the lead. His win looked imminent. Then the unthinkable happened. With a pop Derek's right hamstring muscle tore, and he fell to the ground in agony.

Determined to finish, Derek lifted himself to his feet, his leg quivering, and ever so slowly, hobbled down the track.

Jim, seeing his son in trouble, raced from the top row of the stands, and jumped over the railing. With two security officers chasing after him, he ran to help his son.

Derek waved away the oncoming medical personnel and limped onward, his tear-stained face twisted in agony.

The race now over, the crowd of 65,000 rose to their feet and cheered. The volume grew as Redmond, in searing pain took one painful step at a time.

"I'm here, son," Jim came alongside and hugged his son. "We'll finish together."

Sobbing, Derek placed his arm around his father's shoulders.

Arm in arm, they continued their painful journey. Just before the finish, Jim released Derek to allow him to complete the course on his own. The crowd in total frenzy responded with a standing ovation.

With tears in his eyes, Jim Redmond told the press afterwards, "I'm the proudest father alive. I'm prouder of him than I would have been if he had won the gold medal."

Derek Redmond's name will be remembered long after records are broken, and medals have tarnished. He persevered, and with his father's help, finished strong.

You too have a loving heavenly Father. Just as Derek Redmond's dad ran to his son, the Father runs to meet His children (even when they have wandered far from home, see Luke 15:11-20[13]).

God will never leave or forsake you. He will hold you close through every step, and someday He will welcome you home as you cross the final finish line.

- Using the NASB version, fill in the blanks of Psalm 37:23-24[14]. "The steps of a man are established by the Lord, and He _____ in his way. When he falls, he shall not be hurled headlong, because the Lord is the One who _____ _____ _____."

God delights in you, holds, and upholds you, reassuring you that you don't need to fear, He will help you. Even when you fall, His loving grip keeps you safe.

Have you ever been in a body of water completely panicked, with arms flailing, thinking you're drowning, when in reality all you had to do was lower your feet and stand?

I've been there, done that. Rather embarrassing, but very comforting when those toes touch something solid.

How easy it is to flounder, flap, and flail in the midst of our circumstances. I'll be honest, I can flounder, flap, and flail as well as anyone.

How often do we forget that Jesus promises that no one can snatch us out of His hands or the hands of God the Father? Stop, rest, think about, and relish that wonderful truth. When we take the time to be still, remembering God is in control and we are loved, the flailing stops.

God tells us to cease striving, be still, and know that He is God. "Be still" in Hebrew means to sink down, let drop, be quiet, or relax.

When rescuing a drowning victim, lifeguards need the person to be still, to stop flailing and trust the skills of the rescuer. The calmer the person, the easier the rescue. Fortunately, even in the crashing waves of problems and difficulties, even when flailing and panicked, we can lean back, confident in the palm of God's hands.

No matter what difficulties you face, you really are always safe in God's hands. You are forever firmly planted in His love. The hands which formed you and gave you life, beckons you to relax in the life of His loving hands.

You are always held secure in the Hands of Jesus. No matter where you are, or what is happening, He will never let you fall.

- **What qualities does Paul use to describe God in 2 Corinthians 1:3-5[15]? What does God provide for us?**

- **What does God promise in Isaiah 54:10[16]?**

God is the Father of mercies and the God of all comfort. His lovingkindness remains, His peace is never shaken, and His compassion is forever on you and forever for you.

God is a good, good Father. He cares, He loves, He reaches out and calls to the lost. His heart is tender toward all He has made. There is no problem and no situation too big for our God. There is nothing beyond His reach.

God is just and righteous. Evil will be punished. And someday soon, tears will be wiped away and eternal safety given to His children.

> *"At the end of our meandering, up-hill-down-hill journey there is a loving Father waiting at the end of the pathway that we tread; watching, waiting, with open arms to welcome us back home... The Father's greatest joy is his children coming home."*
> *~ Jack Brewer*

Whatever you face, whatever your need, run to God and remember He is a good, good Father. His arms are open wide to hold you and carry you through. Oh God is such a good, good Father.

- **Linger slow in Psalm 91[17] and make note of the beautiful promises God has given.**

Resting in fellowship

The year was 1958, and Jack, a young seminary student, drove along a cold, rainy highway on the way to an appointment. He noticed an elderly man standing on the side of the road and without a thought Jack "tossed" out a prayer on the man's behalf as he drove past.

When Jack arrived at his destination, he discovered his appointment was not available. In a sour mood he began the journey back home. Again, he passed the man who now was on his side of the road, and Jack found himself annoyed with God for not answering his earlier prayer.

Then it dawned on him, perhaps he was the one who needed to give the man a ride. Half-heartedly Jack stopped and backed the distance to where the man stood waiting.

Cringing, Jack sat in the car wondering if the man would be covered in the stench of alcohol or body odor.

Instead Jack found himself pleasantly surprised, at the clean scent, well-shaven, intelligent man who sat next to him. Thinking perhaps this was an opportunity to witness; Jack turned to his companion to start a conversation. "Lousy weather we're having; isn't it?"

The man smiled kindly, nodded, and looked Jack in the eye. "Son, are you saved?"

The question caught him by surprise, and he sat momentarily dumfounded. Words flowed as Jack shared with the man his faith journey, how he had drifted away from God but was brought back through the sweet faith of the young woman who now was his wife.

The man introduced himself as Mr. Doss and told how he walked with the Lord and witnessed to every person he was "supposed to meet that day." He spoke of the Holy Spirit and the Bible. Mentioning he had memorized most of God's word because his eyesight was not great for reading.

"You know," Mr. Doss said with a smile, "I am so happy that when I pick up my left foot it says, Glory and when I pick up the right it says, Hallelujah!"

Jack surveyed the man. "Aren't you lonely?"

Mr. Doss looked at him with surprise. "How could I be lonely?" He continued to tell Jack of his time in prayer, Bible study, and fellowship with God. "How could I be lonely?"

After they parted company, Jack knew he would never be the same man. To this day he wonders who Mr. Doss really was, especially since on that cold, rainy day, Mr. Doss wasn't even wet.

The story is special to me and my family. Jack is my dad.

Someday I'll meet Mr. Doss and we'll walk the glory, hallelujah golden streets and talk about our wonderful God.

- **According to 1 Corinthians 1:9[18], what are you called into?**
  "God is faithful, through whom you were called into _____ with His Son, Jesus Christ our Lord."

God, who created you, longs to communicate and spend time with you. You were created for fellowship. The Greek and 1828 Shaffer's dictionary defines the word "fellowship" as intimacy, community, social or familiar intercourse, companionship, mutual association of persons on equal and friendly terms.

The fellowship with God is an offering to communicate and commune with the One who made you and loves you. Walking with God is intimacy between Creator and His child.

- **Based on Genesis 5:24[19], what did Enoch accomplish?**

I've always been fascinated with Enoch. Enoch walked with God and walked straight into heaven. I'd like to vote for that, please.

We aren't told Enoch held major revivals, or wrote hundreds of books about God, or he was a major speaker or preacher, but only that he chose to walk with God.

The amazing qualification and mention for Enoch's walk wasn't based on his earthly achievements but on his relationship and fellowship with God.

Isn't it an incredible thought that choosing to walk with God is an ultimate achievement? What's awesome is any one of us can do the same.

No matter who you are, where you live, your health issues, your nationality, your financial status ... you are given the invitation to fellowship and walk with God.

I love the New Living Translation of Psalm 27:8 "My heart has heard you say, *'Come and talk with me.' And my heart responds, 'Lord, I am coming.'*"

The verse is an invitation from The Creator of the universe. Amazing, isn't it? When you are desperate for God's presence, it is God calling you to come to His presence. God is The One who calls.

God already knows your every thought (Psalm 139:2[20]) but still longs for you to talk with Him, to listen, and enjoy His company. If you have given your life to Christ, you are given the ability to talk to Him and hear His voice.

God speaks through His word, through a preacher or Bible teacher, during moments of praise, while enjoying the beauty of His creation, through Godly insight from others, and through Bible studies that bring us closer to His presence.

- **What does God ask us to do in Jeremiah 33:3[21]?**

- **What does Jesus tell us in John 10:27[22]?**

God really does want to talk with you. Take a moment to talk to God, your heavenly Father. God loves you, He loves His children, He cares and He listens.

Tell God your fears, concerns, worries, bring all to Him and know you are free to speak your mind.

God won't ever be surprised about what you tell Him. Remember you are loved exceedingly, abundantly more than you could ask or imagine. As you share your heart with Him, then listen for His response to your heart.

> *"God's voice brings peace. A sure sign that you have heard God's voice is that you are comforted and uplifted - encouraged to love Him, to trust Him and to follow Him." ~ Peter Lord*

God's love, His amazing love, loves you. He wants to spend time with you, talk with you.

Regardless of age, body type, skin color, hair color (dyed, natural, or missing), rich or poor, you are a divine creation. You were created by love, for love, to love, created in the image of our glorious God. You have value because you are His beloved child.

Each snowflake is individually formed; ice crystals that radiate sunlight as they flutter to the ground. You are a beautiful crystal of God's love, created unique for His unique purposes. God's love for you is not dependent on what you do for Him or how you perform.

- **What does Paul share in Ephesians 2:10[23]?**

You are God's purposeful workmanship, work of art, a masterpiece; doesn't that make you want to sit a little taller and walk with a bounce in your step?

Masterpieces have great value. Always remember, you are treasured by the God of the universe.

You have been created by Glory for glory. God has a plan and purpose for your life.

God, your heavenly Father, loves you.

- **According to Revelation 3:20[24], what is God doing and saying?**

Every day, God calls and speaks His love. Unfortunately, in the trials and busyness of the days, hearing is difficult.

Years ago, the company where my husband worked, outsourced his facility and he was laid off. For 448 long, long, long days he searched for new employment. When work finally came, (thinking our Texas house would sell quickly), we gathered up two weeks' worth of clothes, my laptop, our dog, and headed north to Idaho. Ten months later, we continued to wait for our Texas house to sell.

Our temporary apartment was a blessing, but I missed my privacy. I missed a quiet room where I could shut the door and spend time writing and talking with God. I missed my books. I missed my stuff. I wanted a couch that didn't feel like it was stuffed with prairie dog pelts. I wanted things to be different, and I wanted to be settled.

Yes, the pity party had hit with full abandon, and the whine mode clung to my shoulders like a wet rag, and, a wet whining Buffaloe is not a pretty picture.

With my million complaints, I tromped to the kitchen and poured a cup of coffee. Leaning against the counter, I pondered what really was behind my frustrations.

Why was I so unsettled? Why didn't I feel like God was with me? Then in my soul, the still small voice whispered, "***I'm always here.***"

Tears fell as all my complaints sloughed off and fell in a heap to the floor.

I should have known God would never leave.

During difficulties, unwanted life changes, and the craziness of the day, it's easy to allow the mind to whirl with frustrations, whines, and complaints. It's far too easy to wonder in hardships if something is missing, something that keeps us from feeling God is near.

Whining and complaining wasn't the answer for my unsettled soul. However, remembering God's truth, that He will never leave or forsake, and the truth Jesus said, "***I am with you always even to the end of the age***" gives comfort and peace. Because, the truth is that God's love is unfailing, and the truth of any situation is found in God's Truth.

You may feel as though you are all alone, but that is never true. God's promises of His presence, His unfailing love, comfort, hope, and peace abound throughout His word. God's hope, His presence, His love is with you, even to the end of the age.

- **Read the following verses and note God's promises.**

- **Deuteronomy 31:8**[25]

- **Isaiah 43:1-3a**[26]

- **Psalm 33:18**[27]

- **Matthew 28:20**[28]

God's love reaches to the heavens, endures forever, is faithful, just, righteous, merciful, rich, abounding in love, great, everlasting to everlasting, gracious, and compassionate. The love of Christ is wide, long, high, and deep, a love that floods the soul with joy and unfailing love.

- **What does Paul tell us about God's love in Romans 8:38-39**[29]**?**

- **Based on Romans 8:28**[30]**, how many things will God work for good in your life?**

- **According to Luke 1:37**[31]**, what is impossible for God?**

God is trustworthy, He is truth, and His love never fails. Nothing is impossible for Him, and He will make sure all things work out for good.

You may not see it now, you may have to wait some time for the good to come to fruition, but you can be assured God's good plans and purposes will always prevail.

- **Underline or highlight the truths about God in the following verses.**

- "For the word of the Lord holds true, and we can trust everything He does. He loves whatever is just and good; the unfailing love of the Lord fills the earth" Psalm 33:4-5 NLT).

- "The Lord is merciful and gracious, slow to anger and abounding in compassion and lovingkindness" (Psalm 103:8 AMP).

- "The Lord's lovingkindnesses indeed never cease, for His compassions never fail. They are new every morning; great is Your faithfulness. 'The Lord is my portion,' says my soul, therefore I have hope in Him" (Lamentations 3:22-24 NASB).

> *"Think about God as often as you can, day and night, in everything you do. He is always with you. Just as you would be rude if you deserted a friend who was visiting you, why would you be disrespectful of God by abandoning His presence? Do not forget Him! Think of Him often. Adore Him ceaselessly. Live and die with Him. That is the real business of Christians; in a word, it is our profession." ~ Brother Lawrence*

Resting in grace

As a teenager I wondered what the top speed was for my little car. A two-lane farm road afforded the opportunity. I decided to put the pedal to the metal. Yep, I stuck my foot on the gas and flew down the road. That little engine whined and screamed.

But then, I saw the patrol car sitting on the side of the road. I knew I had been caught. My speed had to be obvious. How many little Toyotas whiz by at break-neck speed?

The first opportunity to stop was a gravel road leading to a farmhouse. Feeling very sheepish, I pulled over and waited.

The patrol car stopped behind me, no lights and no siren. The officer just sat in his car. A few minutes later he approached my open window. "Do you live here?"

I kept my hands on the wheel. "No sir."

The officer didn't move. "You just pulled over?"

Nodding, I tried to gauge the officer's reaction. "Yes sir."

His face showed no emotion, his eyes hidden behind mirrored sunglasses. "What were you doing?"

"I was trying to see how fast my car would go."

He didn't move for a few minutes. Finally, he shook his head. "Don't do it again." And with that, he turned and walked away.

I deserved to get a ticket. I even admitted my crime. Although I was guilty, I was pardoned and given the gift of grace.

Two thousand years ago, our Holy God bent down from heaven to offer His grace-filled love through His Son, Jesus Christ. We don't deserve His mercy. Nothing we can do on our own would grant us the right to stand before a pure and Hallowed God.

Forgiveness is our Holy God reaching through the outstretched hands of His precious son Jesus, where all our sins were nailed to the cross. But for the grace of God, we would all be lost.

- **What are we told in Romans 3:23[32]?**

God is a Holy God. Grace offered, and freely given, didn't come without a huge price.

Jesus, the Son of God, fought to the death for you, fought through death for you, for you to have a relationship with God, The Father.

- **According to Romans 5:8[33] what did God and Jesus do?**

God made a way for God's grace before we even knew we needed His grace. Through the love of God and His Son, Jesus Christ we have the forgiveness of sins.

> *"The only ground on which God can forgive our sin and reinstate us to His favor is through the Cross of Christ. There is no other way! Forgiveness, which is so easy for us to accept, cost the agony at Calvary. We should never take the forgiveness of sin, the gift of the Holy Spirit, and our sanctification in simple faith, and then forget the enormous cost to God that made all of this ours. Forgiveness is the divine miracle of grace. The cost to God was the Cross of Christ. To forgive sin, while remaining a holy God, this price had to be paid."*
> *~ Oswald Chambers*

God's grace, which is rooted in His great love for us, is truly amazing. Not one of us is good enough to receive it. Likewise, not one of us is bad enough to *not* receive it. God offers His grace through His Son, Jesus. God's grace, amazing grace, is BIG enough for us all.

Please don't think for a minute you've fallen too far from God's mercy and love, or that you are so good you don't need God's mercy and love. We are all in need of a Savior, and that Savior (Jesus) can fill every need.

- **According to Philippians 4:19[34], what are you supplied? How many needs will be met?**

- **Read the verses below and underline the amazing gifts and blessings you are given through Jesus Christ.**

    "Blessed is the God and Father of our Lord Jesus Christ, who has blessed us with every spiritual blessing in the heavenly realms in Christ. For he chose us in Christ before the foundation of the world that we may be holy and unblemished in his sight in love. He did this by predestining us to adoption as his sons through Jesus Christ, according to the pleasure of his will—to the praise of the glory of his grace that he has freely bestowed on us in his dearly loved Son. In him we have redemption through his blood, the forgiveness of our trespasses, according to the riches of his grace that he lavished on us in all wisdom and insight. He did this when he revealed to us the secret of his will, according to his good pleasure that he set forth in Christ, toward the administration of the fullness of the times, to head up all things in Christ—the things in heaven and the things on earth. In Christ we too have been claimed as God's own possession, since we were predestined according to the one purpose of him who accomplishes all things according to the counsel of his will so that we, who were the first to set our hope on Christ, would be to the praise of his glory. And when you heard the word of truth (the gospel of your salvation)—when you believed in Christ—you were marked with the seal of the promised Holy Spirit, who is the down payment of our inheritance, until the redemption of God's own possession, to the praise of his glory" (Ephesians 1:3-14 NET).

"We thank God for His loving-favor to us. He gave this loving favor to us through His much-loved Son. Because of the blood of Christ, we are bought and made free from the punishment of sin. And because of His blood, our sins are forgiven. His loving favor to us is so rich. He was so willing to give all of this to us. He did this with wisdom and understanding" (Ephesians 1:6-8 NLV).

The verses in Ephesians reveals God's lavish, amazing love. God has blessed you with every spiritual blessing in Christ. He lovingly chose you before the foundation of the world so that you would be holy and unblemished in His sight. You are adopted as His child through Jesus Christ according to the pleasure of His will. You are redeemed through His Son, His grace lavished on you with all wisdom and insight through His good pleasure. You are God's praise and glory, marked with the seal of the Holy Spirit.

> *"The fathomless love of the Saviour's heart is every drop of it ours; every sinew in the arm of might, every jewel in the crown of majesty, the immensity of divine knowledge, and the sternness of divine justice, all are ours, and shall be employed for us. The whole of Christ, in His adorable character as the Son of God, is by Himself made over to us most richly to enjoy. His wisdom is our direction, his knowledge our instruction, his power our protection, his justice our surety, his love our comfort, his mercy our solace, and his immutability our trust. He makes no reserve but opens the recesses of the Mount of God and bids us dig in its mines for the hidden treasures."*
> *~ Charles Spurgeon*

The gift of grace, the gift of Jesus, is eternal treasure deeper, wider, richer than anyone can imagine. Read Spurgeon's quote again, replace "us" with "you," "ours" with "yours," and read his words knowing this lavish gift is truly yours.

- **In Hebrews 4:15-16[35], what assurances are given that Jesus will understand your needs? What will you find when you come to Him?**

Jesus knows, understands, and cares. He walked the dusty roads of this earth and experienced everything you experience.

Jesus knows what it feels like to be rejected, hurt, to lose loved ones, to see the terrible effects of sin, and He knows how much life hurts.

Whatever you face, Jesus understands. He is there for you and He is with you to help you through every moment of your life.

Jesus, God in flesh, holy, perfect and pure, Immanuel – God with us. The Great I Am is with you. Christ Jesus, the Savior, brought a hands-on relationship to a fallen world. Approachable and touchable, Jesus allowed intimacy and closeness from His disciples and other people. Jesus took little children into His arms and blessed them.

Jesus touched the lame, the poor, the diseased, the outcasts and those deemed untouchable.

Jesus hurts when you hurt. He weeps when you weep. The God of all compassion moves toward you in your pain, heartache and suffering. He is near to the broken-hearted. He raises dead hearts back to life. Jesus calms the storms. He is a very present help in times of trouble, and He is present with you in your trouble. An amazing verse in John 21:20 gives insight in the blessings you have in Jesus.

- **According to John 21:20[36], what had John, the beloved disciple, been doing during the meal?**

John had leaned against the chest of God-in-flesh. As a follower of Jesus, you are given the same invitation. Your heart is made to crave God, because you are created by God for fellowship with God, and that offer is as intimate as resting against His chest.

Oh my, what a blessing that God through His Son invites you to lean against His chest.

- **Based on Romans 8:14-17[37], what other benefits are you given through Christ?**

> *"All the attributes of Christ, as God and man, are at our disposal. All the fulness of the Godhead, whatever that marvelous term may comprehend, is ours to make us complete. He cannot endow us with the attributes of Deity; but he has done all that can be done, for he has made even his divine power and Godhead subservient to our salvation. His omnipotence, omniscience, omnipresence, immutability and infallibility, are all combined for our defence."*
> *~ Charles Spurgeon*

The invitation of God to be brought into His family – adopted with the same benefits of a birth child, with the benefits given through His Son, Jesus Christ. You are given a love relationship with pure and perfect loving intimacy. You are adopted with the tender intimacy of your Father as His beloved child.

- **What did Jesus call His disciples in John 15:15[38]?**

Such amazing, beautiful, incredible blessings we are given through Jesus Christ. No situation, no sin, no person, no government, NOTHING can stop the power of Jesus Christ within His followers.

In Jesus "all the fullness of Deity (the Godhead) dwells in bodily form [completely expressing the divine essence of God]. And **in Him you have been made complete** [achieving spiritual stature through Christ], and He is the head over all rule and authority [of every angelic and earthly power]" (Colossians 2:9-10 AMP).

Please remember, if you are in Christ...

> you are forgiven.
> you are eternally secure and soul-safe.
> you are free in Christ.
> you are never alone.
> you are loved now and forever.
> you have access to God.
> you have hope forever.
> and, you always get a happy ending.

Living life with Jesus Christ is the safest place to live your life. Our pastor reminded our church that if we are in Christ Jesus we are like Noah when he was inside the ark.

Noah was safe and secure, even in the storms, even in the driving rain, even if Noah tripped and fell, even if he was wobbly on his feet, even if he wondered if the storm would ever end, even if he wondered if God would remember him and his family, Noah was safe in the ark.

Even when you feel so small, when the storms are raging and you're so very wobbly on your faith-feet, even when you're tripping and falling, you are always safe in Christ.

Your unlimited need is always matched by the unlimited grace of God.

Rest in the complete, resurrection, restoring, redeeming, friendship, grace-filled power of Jesus Christ living within you.

Let's give "thanks to the Father, who has qualified us to share in the inheritance of the saints in Light. For He rescued us from the domain of darkness and transferred us to the kingdom of His beloved Son, in whom we have redemption, the forgiveness of sins" (Colossians 1:12-14 NASB).

> *"The Lord Jesus is perfectly confident that He can meet our needs and He would have us confident too; for He is the One who for thousands of years has met the needs of those who put their trust in Him."* ~ L. B. Cowman[39]

Session Two

Come aside and rest

I sat at my computer looking at updates online. Some shared highlights of their day, photos of themselves and family members, Bible verses, fun graphics or videos. Unfortunately, also mixed in were news reports, rants and frustrations of the state of our country and our world. I felt my soul sinking, dazed at the negativity, anger, and hopelessness.

A quiet voice within me beckoned, "***Come away.***"

Surprised I had a choice, I sat stunned. Troubles and distractions are so troublesome and distracting, they pull, claw at us to pay attention to the neediness of the needs.

Even Jesus often withdrew to a quiet place. Even in the clamor of the world around Him, Jesus made time, took time to step away.

There is an art of stepping away, walking away, to get back in step to walk with The One who is The Way.

Like athletes who sit on the bench after a big play and suck down oxygen, we need to breathe the Breath of Life.

We need to look away from the world and look up to The One who created the world. Jesus beckons, "***Come away.***"

- **According to Matthew 11:28[40], where do you find rest?**

- **What did Jesus tell His disciples in Mark 6:31[41]?**

Come aside and rest.

You find soul-filling for parched souls, and you find soul-rest in God's presence.

- **Read again Matthew 11:28-30[42]. What are the actions Jesus asks you to do?**

For most of my life, taking a yoke (even if it is easy) didn't sound very restful. I visualized a large ox yoked with a smaller ox; the large beast doing the majority of the work while the little one strained and struggled to stay in step.

However, the Lord blessed with a visual that makes much more sense. Jesus, the Son of God, the Prince of Peace, stands tall with the yoke across His mighty shoulders. I stand next to Him, tiny against His powerful presence. The cords that bind me to His yoke drift down, light and easy. My feet barely touch the ground as Jesus moves forward. I'm swinging, swaying, rejoicing to be led by Him. He carries the burden, He shoulders every hardship and difficulty.

The only times the yoke is heavy is when I pull ahead or strain to maneuver and do things my way.

> *"True rest to the mind of the child of God is rest on the wing, rest in motion, rest in service, not rest with the yoke off, but with the yoke on." ~ Charles Spurgeon*

I love the MSG version of Matthew 11:28-30, "Come to me. Get away with me and you'll recover your life. **I'll show you how to take a real rest. Walk with me and work with me—watch how I do it. Learn the unforced rhythms of grace.** I won't lay anything heavy or ill-fitting on you. Keep company with me and you'll learn to live freely and lightly."

Yes, yes, yes! Keep company with Jesus, walk with Him, abide, dwell, remain, live and move and have your being in the rhythm of God's presence and grace. Put His yoke on and watch how Jesus lived. Jesus brings real rest as you abide in His unforced rhythms of grace.

- **Underline or highlight the word "abide" in the following passage.**

    "I am the vine, you are the branches. He who abides in Me, and I in him, bears much fruit; for without Me you can do nothing. If you abide in Me, and My words abide in you, you will ask what you desire, and it shall be done for you. As the Father loved Me, I also have loved you; abide in My love. If you keep My commandments, you will abide in My love, just as I have kept My Father's commandments and abide in His love. These things I have spoken to you, that My joy may remain in you, and that your joy may be full" (John 15:5, 7, 9-11 NKJV).

The Strong's Greek definition of the word "Abide" G3306 is to remain, abide, to sojourn, tarry, not to depart, to continue to be present, **to be held**, kept, continually, to continue to be, not to perish, to last, endure, to remain as one, not to become another or different, to wait for, await one.

Abiding in Jesus, abiding in The Father, is an invitation to be held in the love of Jesus and the love of the Father.

- **What does Jesus promise in John 15:11[43] when you abide in His love?**

Abiding is a beautiful word.

Abiding is a word by The Word inviting you to rest, dwell, tarry or stay for a short time, to be firm and immovable, to remain and continue, not to depart, to be held, kept continually, to remain as one.

No matter how busy your life, you can abide in The One who is life.

I studied a photo of a woman who sat still, her back to the photographer. In front of her was a beautiful garden. The picture evoked serenity, and I'll admit to being a touch jealous of her and her location. Then it hit me, I too can rest like she rested. With Jesus, it's not about location or the position of our bodies, but a conscious choice to abide with Him.

Your soul is never confined; you have the beautiful reality of being able to commune with God at any moment of the day or night. Even in the rush of things that need to be done, your soul can quietly snuggle up to your Savior. Abiding is stopping while the world continues to whirl. As Jesus holds you, He molds you into His perfect love.

> *"The spirit is the spring of rest, as for the outward surroundings they are of small account. Let but your mind be like the mind of Christ, and you shall find rest unto your souls: a deep rest, a growing rest, a rest found out more and more, an abiding rest, not only which you have found, but which you shall go on to find. Justification gave you rest from the burden of sin, sanctification will give you rest from molesting cares; and in proportion as it becomes perfect, and you are like your Saviour, your rest shall become more like that of heaven."*
> ~ Charles Spurgeon

Come away, come aside and rest...

Picture the most beautiful view of nature you have ever seen. Perhaps a sunset bathed in color, a majestic mountain, a white sand beach with turquoise water, the stars twinkling at midnight. What makes your heart smile?

Picture that place, that perfect place, and now picture Jesus, smiling and loving you, sitting next to you.

Come away, come aside and rest...

"**Come to Me**, all who are weary and heavily burdened ..., and **I will give you rest [refreshing your souls** ... for I am gentle and humble in heart, and you will find rest (renewal, blessed quiet) for your souls" (Matthew 11:28-29 AMP).

> *"Rest is not a hallowed feeling that comes over us in church; it is the repose of the heart set deep in God."* ~ Henry Drummond

Resting in forgiveness

> *"To be a Christian means to forgive the inexcusable, because God has forgiven the inexcusable in you." ~ C. S. Lewis*

In 1947, Holocaust survivor Corrie Ten Boom traveled to Munich to preach about God's forgiveness. Most of her talks were met by silence. But this time, a heavy-set man walked toward her. And then, she realized he had been one of the guards at the concentration camp where she and her sister had been, the very place her sister had died.

The man stood in front of her, his hand thrust out, as he complimented her on the message. It was the first time since her release she had been face-to-face with her captors, and her blood seemed to freeze in her veins. He did not remember her, but she remembered him. He told Corrie he became a Christian and knew God forgave him for all the cruel things he did in the past.

He again extended his hand and asked for her forgiveness.

Corrie didn't move. She knew God required us to forgive in order to receive forgiveness. She had seen proof in her own life and the lives of those in the home she had established for those abused by the Nazis.

Corrie wrote, "Since the end of the war I had a home in Holland for victims of Nazi brutality. Those who were able to forgive their former enemies were able also to return to the outside world and rebuild their lives, no matter what the physical scars. Those who nursed bitterness remained invalids. It was as simple and as horrible as that."

The victims who forgave their enemies were able to heal and return to their lives. The ones who did not forgive, who remained in bitterness, remained invalids.

Corrie realized forgiveness is not an emotion and something to be done regardless of feelings. She prayed silently asking Jesus to help her, and woodenly she thrust her hand in his. And as she did, a current ran down her shoulder and into their joined hands.

At that moment she said she had never felt God's love as intensely as she did then.

- **According to Ephesians 2:8[44], what is grace?**

Forgiveness is a blessing, a gift, an opportunity **for you** to experience God's love on an amazingly intense level.

When God tells you to forgive others, He is not questioning the reality of your wounds, the level of your pain, or that you have been sinned against. Forgiveness is not what you do for them; forgiving others is a gift to yourself.

With the gift of forgiveness comes your freedom, peace of mind, and right fellowship and relationship with God.

Forgiveness does not release their debt. Forgiveness of others releases our debt. With forgiveness, comes **your** freedom, your healing, and your soul-rest.

- **Read Luke 23:33-34a[45], what happened to Jesus, what did He say?**

Jesus, without sin, was falsely accused and condemned, beaten beyond recognition, spat upon, mocked, had thorns driven into His skull via a thorny crown, and then crucified on a cross. While on the cross, looking at those who mocked and scorned Him, those who rejected Him and had beaten Him, and asked The Father to forgive. Jesus offered unmerited unwarranted and undeserving grace.

- **What does Jesus tell us in Matthew 6:14-15?[46]**

Forgiveness comes as you forgive.

After a woman's only son was killed, she was consumed with grief, bitterness, and hate. She prayed, "God, reveal his killer."

Later, she dreamed she was going to heaven, but in order to get there she had to pass through a certain house.

She needed to walk down the street, enter the house through the front door, go through each room, up the stairs, and exit the back door.

She prayed again and asked God whose house this was. His answer, "It's the house of the man who killed your son."

The road to heaven passed through the house of her enemy.

Two nights later, a knock sounded on her front door. She opened the door, and in front of her stood a young man about her late son's age.

He identified himself. "I am the one who killed your son. Since that day, I have had no life. No peace. So here I am, my life is in your hands. Kill me; I am dead already. Have me thrown in jail; I am in prison already. Have me tortured; I am in torment already. Do with me as you wish."

The woman had prayed so long to know who killed her son, but now she found she couldn't kill this young man. She didn't want him thrown in jail or tortured. She only asked one thing. "Come into my home and live with me. Eat the food I would have prepared for my son. Wear the clothes I would have made for my son. Become the son I lost."

And so, he did."[47]

What stands in your way on your road to heaven?

I understand the need and the power of forgiveness. I was raised in a Christian home by parents who loved one another and loved the Lord. However, no one knew (including my parents) what was happening behind the scenes. I was molested by a babysitter, assaulted by two guys in high school, chased by a man with a knife in a parking lot, had a shotgun pointed at me as two men tried to run me off the road, and I've been raped by a doctor. I've been drugged by a nurse and locked up, divorced, stalked, had cancer, and experienced the loss of family and friends to death. I've had eight major surgeries, numerous medical procedures, and over eleven years of chronic illness.

I have made mistakes and had many failures. I've needed to forgive others and forgive myself. I have wounds inside and out, scars from falls and bumps and bruises of life, scars from surgeon knives, and scars from self-inflicted attempts to rid the hurt inside.

You too have your wounds. I'm so sorry. I'm sorry for what life has done to you. My heart aches for you. I don't have a magic potion, enough hugs, or love enough to fix anyone's problems, but I do know a loving, healing, restoring God. I know what He does with broken, messed up, wounded lives. I've seen how God has restored my life and those I'm blessed to have met along the way. God's gentle touch and unfailing love restores and transforms everything the enemy meant for evil to turn it into good.

God tells us to forgive; we must do so – regardless of the sin. He has forgiven us, we must forgive others. The world responds there is justification in not forgiving, or that God is callous by requiring forgiveness, but please remember your forgiveness of others **does not** excuse their sin. Your forgiveness does not make their sin null and void—they still have to stand before God. God does not forget their sin when you forgive them.

When Jesus died on the cross, He said to the Father, "Unto You I commit My spirit" (Luke 23:46). Forgiveness is an act of yielding. It is saying to God, "Unto You I commit the wrong committed against me." It is giving over, yielding to God, so you can live free, and rise from the ashes of your past.

Picture a courtroom. The jury is in place, the lawyers are ready, and the judge sits on the bench. The person who wronged you is brought in. You jump to your feet and you hit that person over and over again. They deserve punishment. They didn't give you mercy, and you show no mercy.

The bailiff and lawyers try to restrain you, but to no avail. You scream and point at the offender, "They do not deserve forgiveness."

The judge bangs his gavel and pronounces his verdict, "As you have spoken, so it will be done. If that person doesn't deserve forgiveness, neither do you."

The choices are limited. We can forgive others and be forgiven. Or we can keep a tally of their sins. The problem is, our sins continue to be tallied. Which sin do you want remaining on your record?

The person most hurt by not forgiving is you.

If you don't forgive, you remain chained to your offender, continually offended by that offense, and that experience. When you refuse to forgive, when you continue to wallow in the wrongs committed to you, you are refusing the blood of the lamb—the blood that is deep enough, red enough, cleansing enough, to heal and erase the hurt, the anger, and the frustrations.

Forgive and release it to God. Not part, not just a little, but all. You can be chained to your heartache and your unforgiving spirit or you can be released today.

God will punish the guilty. No sin goes unnoticed. Repeat that. No. Sin. Goes. Unnoticed. God knows everything they did and thought. He knows what we did and did not do.

- **What does Proverbs 15:3[48] tell us?**

- **What does Jesus say in Matthew 10:26[49]?**

- **According to Isaiah 13:11[50], what will God do?**

God keeps watch on the wicked and the good. Jesus promises, there is nothing covered that will not be revealed, and hidden that will not be known. God will punish the guilty.

Unfortunately, I know a person still angry at someone who has been dead for decades. Anger has done nothing but stagnate their growth—causing bitterness, illness, and a lack of connection with those around them. I have seen people turn into a version of the very person they hated, because that is what consumed them -- that is who they thought about, and that is who they became.

> *"When you deal intimately with human beings...you wonder at times if forgiveness is not as rare as hen's teeth. People bury hatchets but carefully tuck away the map which tells where their hidden weapon lies. We put our resentments in cold storage and then pull the switch to let them thaw out again. Our grudges are taken out to the lake to drown them—even the lake of prayer—and we end up giving them a swimming lesson. How often have we torn up the canceled note but hung on to the wastebasket that holds the pieces?" — Lofton Hudson*

An unforgiving spirit fouls up everything—including attitudes, and relationships with others and with God. The garbage of unforgiveness is heavy, depressing, smelly, stinky, and rots from the inside out.

- **According to Hebrews 12:15, underline what happens if unforgiveness and bitterness remain in your life.**

    "Exercise foresight and be on the watch to look [after one another], to see that no one falls back from and fails to secure God's grace (His unmerited favor and spiritual blessing), in order that no root of resentment (rancor, bitterness, or hatred) shoots forth and causes trouble and bitter torment, and the many become contaminated and defiled by it" (Hebrews 12:15 AMPC).

- **What advice is given in Ephesians 4:26-27?**[51]

Through Christ, you find the power to forgive and through Him you receive your healing. Release your burden to God -- not part, not just a little, but all. You can be chained to your heartache and your unforgiving spirit, or you can be released today.

Let's replay the courtroom scenario. The date arrives and the person who wronged you appears before the judge. You forgive—not because the person deserves forgiveness—you forgive because Christ has forgiven you. The judge listens quietly and pronounces his verdict. The person who wronged you is convicted. With a righteous Judge, the punishment always fits the crime.

Jesus has given a key to freedom, and forgiveness is the ax that cuts you free. Jesus reaches out with compassion, mercy, and grace. Forgive, and you will be forgiven. Justice is served, and you walk free.

When you forgive, the chain that binds you to that person is cut. Forgiveness unlocks the chains that chained you. As you forgive, the chains that tie you, and the negative thoughts and emotions, lose their hold so you can float free. The person remains chained to their sin, but you go free.

Jesus willingly went to the cross for you, taking your sins and cleansing you through His grace and mercy. His love paid the price, love that caught you by the hand and saved you for a wonderful, eternal life.

Paul wrote that love is patient, kind, not jealous; love does not brag, it is not arrogant. It does not act disgracefully, it does not seek its own benefit; is not provoked, doesn't keep an account of a wrong suffered, doesn't rejoice in unrighteousness, but rejoices with the truth; love keeps every confidence, believes all things, hopes all things, endures all things and love never fails (1 Corinthians 13:1-8). God's love is big enough, patient enough, kind enough, and grace-filled enough to cover all your sin.

Come to Christ and allow your soul to rest in the beauty of God's loving forgiveness.

The Rest of forgiveness

Sometimes forgiving others is easier than forgiving ourselves. My sins and failures are many. I'm horrified and embarrassed at some of the choices I made in the past. Temptation presented itself as an ocean of delight. I stood on the edge thinking perhaps I could dip just a toe in and no one would notice, and surely no one would get hurt.

However, at the slightest step, I found myself over my head covered in the mud of slimy sin. Nothing could remove those stains. Nothing and no one, except the mercy and grace of Jesus.

Don't let the enemy convince you that your sin is too bad, too many, or too terrible for God's forgiveness. Or, that you have to get your life in order and get yourself clean before you can be saved or useful in God's kingdom.

The devil (or our own conscience) replays failures over and over again or others won't allow us to move on and forget. But remember you don't need to fear or run and hide because God knows about every sin, every thought, and every action that you have done. He knows about your yesterday, today, and tomorrow, and still He offers grace and mercy.

I've heard people say that because of their sins there is no hope for repair or restoration. Consequences do exist for our sin; however, God is bigger than any mistake or failure.

- **David was an adulterer and murderer, but what did God call him based on Acts 12:22?** [52]

- **Moses killed a man, but how did God talk with Moses according to Exodus 33:11?** [53]

- **Rahab was a prostitute, but whose lineage is she listed in Matthew 1:5-17?** [54]

Saul/Paul stood by watching and agreeing with the stoning of Steven and then he persecuted Christians, but God used Paul in mighty ways to further His kingdom.

- **What did Jesus say in John 8:7 to those who brought the woman caught in adultery for stoning?** [55]

The only one without sin who could have thrown a stone, instead gave grace. The sinless One offers grace to the sinner.

Peter denied Christ three times. The resurrected Christ gave Peter three times to affirm his love and then told him to feed His sheep. Basically, Peter was told, "you're forgiven, move on, you have a job to do."

Regardless of your past, no matter what has happened, what you have been through, God's forgiveness is freely offered for those who come to Him. Let that steep in you. The Lord will forgive if you honestly, earnestly confess, and repent.

Grace touches to the very marrow of your being and cleanses from the inside out, creating a new creature in Christ. Created uniquely, you become the best you can be through His grace. All you must do is accept what He so freely offers.

That thing you did, the thing that was done to you, the shame you feel. The terrible feeling, the nightmares, the heaviness of guilt. Satan wants you to keep those negative feelings, carry those burdens, and wallow in the past all of your days. I want you to know the truth. Jesus brings good news and is The Good News. You do not have to carry what God has freed you from.

Jesus gives freedom from the past, freedom for today, and freedom for eternity. It is for freedom that Christ set you free.

Whatever is taken to Christ is washed, restored, and renewed.

Your sins have been forgiven and are as far as the east is from the west (Psalm 103:12), therefore there is no condemnation for those who are in Christ Jesus (Romans 8:1).

You don't have to carry guilt or shame. I've had some rotten things done to me, and I've done some rotten things. Satan tries to hit me with a variety of past failures and difficulties. I have taken my sins to Jesus and repented and have been forgiven. The things others have done to me, I've carried to Jesus and He has healed my broken heart and bound my wounds.

God has taken what the enemy meant for evil and used for good, and Jesus will do the same for you.

Regardless of what you have done or others have done to you, there is no sin too big for God to forgive, and there is no shame that is too heavy for God to shoulder.

Jesus despised the shame of the cross yet took our sins and shame and nailed them there, and by His sacrifice we are washed clean. Jesus conquered sin and death and rose again to give us new life free of guilt and shame. Don't listen to the enemy's lies that you need to keep living in failure, shame, and guilt. Every one of your sins paid on the cross by the sacrifice of Jesus. His grace covers you.

Forgiveness is a Holy God reaching out through the outstretched hands of His precious son Jesus, where all your sins were nailed to the cross. A lifetime could be lost in striving for unachievable perfection, but God's forgiveness is instantaneous. Jesus stands at the door of your freedom; Jesus is The Door to your freedom.

The Old Idaho State Penitentiary first opened its doors in 1870 and continued to operate until 1973. During the years of operation, the prison housed 13,000 convicts, one of which was Harry Orchard. Orchard began his sentence in 1908 after being convicted of the assassination of a former governor of Idaho.

Years later, due to good behavior, Orchard was offered parole. He chose to stay and eventually died on April 13, 1954.

Our tour guide surmised perhaps the man had enemies on the outside he didn't want to face, or after serving so long in prison, he couldn't imagine leaving.

After parole was offered, Harry chose to return to his dingy cell, never again to experience freedom. He had a choice. You also have a choice.

Many people are locked in their past. Innocence was taken from them, or through their own bad choices innocence was lost. Unable to move forward, they remain trapped in the prison of their mind. Memories pounce and mangle leaving them shaking, quaking, unable to process what happened, much less deal with today.

How can you regain what was lost? How can you go free when your enemies continue to roam or your own failures condemn? The enemy pushes you inside the prison but can't lock you in. Jesus stands at the door to your freedom.

- **In Luke 4:18[56], what did Jesus say He come to do?**

Jesus came to set the captives free and to release the prisoners. If you choose freedom, you go through Christ to be washed clean.

- **What assurances are you given in 1 John 1:9?[57]**

- **What factual hope is given in 1 John 3:2-3?[58]**

Jesus, your High Priest, stands at the door.

- **Underline the promises found in this passage...** "and since we have a great priest over the house of God, let us draw near with a sincere heart in full assurance of faith, having our hearts sprinkled clean from an evil conscience and our bodies washed with pure water. Let us hold fast the confession of our hope without wavering, for He who promised is faithful" (Hebrews 10:21-23 NASB).

Through Jesus Christ, the perfect Lamb of God, the Lamb without blemish, cleanses your heart and soul, innocence is regained, and new life is given.

- **According to Isaiah 1:18[59], what happens when we give our sins to God?**

- **Based on 2 Corinthians 5:17[60] what happens when we give our lives to Christ?**

Please visualize the process. God offers total and complete restoration. You chose Christ, and every bad thought, every evil action, every evil touch, are taken away. Every bit of sin is forgiven and removed, every spot now pure. You are wholly recreated in Christ. When God looks at you, He sees His perfect Son.

Your prison cell is open and you are free. Again, Jesus stands at the door, this time to block the path back to the past. Jesus, His heart filled with love, compassion, and mercy, stands at the door.

Those bad memories? You don't have to go back, Jesus stands at the door.

Those failures? They're gone, Jesus stands at the door.

Your sins? They're clean, Jesus stands at the door.

Don't listen to Satan's lies that you can never be free, or your innocence never regained. Don't believe the enemy who was behind all the evil in the first place. The cell door is open and Jesus stands at the door.

You are completely, totally, washed clean, innocence restored, recreated and free in Christ.

- **According to Psalm 103:12 what does God do with your forgiven sins?[61]**

God forgives and throws your sins as far as the east is to the west and remembers them no more.

God beckons, "I have swept away your sins like a cloud. I have scattered your offenses like the morning mist. Oh, return to me, for I have paid the price to set you free" (Isaiah 44:22 NLT).

- **If you still are having trouble forgiving. Read Psalm 146:7.[62] What promise does God make for the oppressed and those who are imprisoned?**

- **Perhaps you really want to tell your offender how much they hurt you, how wrong they were, and you would really like them to hurt like you did. What does Romans 12:19[63] say?**

- **Perhaps you feel too weak to forgive. What promises are found in Psalm 29:11[64] and Philippians 4:13?[65]**

- **Perhaps you are afraid to forgive. What does Jesus promise in John 14:27?[66]**

- **Perhaps sorrow is overwhelming. Read Psalm 56:8[67] and Isaiah 43:19[68]**

God understands your pain, He cares so much that every tear you cry is precious to Him. God understands your sorrow and grief.

> *"If your past feels like a wilderness, know that God wants to make a road through it, perhaps to help you navigate the difficult years and salvage the good. If your past feels like a desertland of death, know that God will make rivers of redemption flow as He brings beauty out of ashes. Embrace the fresh beginning God wants to give you." ~ Henry Blackaby[69]*

- **Underline the promise given in Romans 8:28.**

    "And we know [with great confidence] that God [who is deeply concerned about us] causes all things to work together [as a plan] for good for those who love God, to those who are called according to His plan and purpose" (Romans 8:28 AMP).

God is enough. He is greater than the past and greater than any trouble. God will take what the enemy meant for evil and turn it into good. God understands. He cares. He has the ears, the arms, the legs, the strength, the might, the justice, the vengeance, the counsel, the comfort, the healing, the peace, the joy, and the life everlasting.

Forgive and rest in the gift and blessing of His grace-filled forgiveness.

Please read the prayer below and fill in the blanks as God leads.

Heavenly Father, I come to You in praise and thanksgiving. Thank You for Your grace and mercy. Thank You for Your Son, Jesus Christ who went to the cross for my sins. Thank You for making a way for me to be forgiven so that I may come to You and be with You forever.

Father, I'm struggling to forgive...
_____.

You are our refuge and strength, a very present help in trouble (Psalm 46:1). Father I run to Your refuge and strength and ask for Your help to forgive.

In my distress I called upon the Lord and cried to my God for help; He heard my voice out of His temple, and my cry for help before Him came into His ears (Psalm 18:6). Thank You, Father.

God, for me this seems impossible, but all things are possible for You (Matthew 19:26).

Righteousness and justice are the foundation of Your throne; lovingkindness and truth go before You (Psalm 89:14).

Therefore, I trust that in Your lovingkindness, You will do what is right and just.

You say, as I forgive, I will be forgiven (Matthew 6:14). Even though it's hard to understand how forgiveness frees me, I so want to be free. I want to be forgiven and I want to be free.

God, I come to You and give You...
_____ _____

I forgive, Father. I forgive.

Thank You, God. Thank You for setting me free.

I ask these things in the name of Jesus Christ, who is my Savior.

Amen.

Beyond the scars

I felt a tug on my soul as though God's unseen hand beckoned me to spend time with Him. I knelt in front of our fireplace with my Bible. While I was praying, I sensed a need to polish our coffee table. I'm easily distracted, but this seemed different. The table looked fine, yet there was an almost playful thought that this urge was more than a cleaning project.

So, I started rubbing the wood with polish and a cloth. As I worked, truths became clear. The wood is beautiful, but the imperfections add character. The knots, rings, and scars formed by growth, environment, hardships, and trials bring beauty. The imperfections deepen and add a richness and glow.

Scars tell of the journey.

I have scars from my head to my toes, some scars have funny stories, some do not, and they all changed me.

Life leaves scars. Internal and external marks of what we've been through. Those scars are precious. They are proof of survival during the fires of life. They are rich, deep, and strengthening.

Scars glow with the testimonies of God's faithfulness, because no matter how deep the scars, God's love runs deeper and His love turns everything into beauty.

Jesus "was pierced for our transgressions, he was crushed for our iniquities; the punishment that brought us peace was on him, and by his wounds we are healed" (Isaiah 53:5 NIV).

Scars tell the most precious story—the story of Jesus and His sacrifice for you. His scars prove His love for you. The scars of Jesus prove your life was worth the suffering to save your life.

Your scars also tell a story. If you will allow God's healing, your scars become a testimony to yourself and others of the beauty of God's love. Your scars are beautiful when you allow Jesus into your scars.

> *"In my deepest wound,*
> *I saw Your glory and it dazzled me."*
> *~ St. Augustine*

May I share hope with you? Kintsugi is the Japanese art of repairing broken pottery with lacquer dusted or mixed with powdered gold, silver, or platinum. What was broken is repaired with precious metal. What was broken becomes a work of art. What was shattered now glows with beauty.

Are you broken?

When you take your broken pieces, your shattered heart and life to God, His restoration glows through with His healing. Nothing is too hard for God, no life is too shattered for God, nothing is impossible for God. God's mending, restoration, and renewal, weaves a golden bond as the goodness of God, the tender mercies of God, heals the broken-hearted and binds wounds.

Become a shining one, a glowing one, by allowing God to heal your wounds and scars. Let God take what the enemy meant for evil and turn it to good. Allow God's healing, light-filled restoration to shine in you and through you. For through the broken, God's light shines.

> *"Do you know the lovely fact about the opal: that in the first place, it is made of desert dust, sand and silica, and owes its beauty and preciousness to a defect? It is a stone with a broken heart. It is full of minute fissures, which admit air, and the air refracts the light. Hence, its lovely hues and that sweet 'lamp of fire' that ever burns at its heart, for the breath of the Lord is in it. You are only conscious of the cracks and desert sand, but so He makes His precious opals. We must be broken in ourselves before we can give back the lovely hues of His light, and the lamp of the Temple can burn in us and never go out."*
> *~ Ellice Hopkins*[70]

- **What comfort is given in Psalm 147:3[71] and Malachi 4:2[72]?**

- **Underline the promises in Romans 8:28. How many things will God work for the good?**

    "And we know [with great confidence] that God [who is deeply concerned about us] causes all things to work together [as a plan] for good for those who love God, to those who are called according to His plan and purpose" (Romans 8:28 AMP).

> *"In a thousand trials, it is not just five hundred of them that work 'for the good' of the believer, but nine hundred and ninety-nine, plus one." ~ George Müller*

Remember the story of Joseph? He was sold into slavery by his brothers, falsely accused of assault, imprisoned for years, and then God elevated him to be second in command under Pharaoh.

- **What did Joseph tell his brothers in Genesis 50:20?**[73]

Joseph's life, what happened to him, and his ultimate rescue, continues to save lives. His story gives hope that even when bad things happen, good will come. The Bible contains true-life situations and true-life rescues.

Your story will be part of a divine rescue that ripples wider than you can imagine. God never wastes your time or your pain. ***Never.***

God's plans are so much bigger than you can imagine or even see. Afflictions, adversities, trials, troubles, and suffering, drive us to our knees and straight to God's heart, for in His loving heart we find all we need.

God is the great architect; His perfect plan never changes. No matter what happens, His plans hold firm and true.

Through the fires of life, through the pain, the highs and lows, the loss and the gain, God refines us and draws us closer to His heart. As He works with us, and through us, more will come to know Him.

- **Based on Psalm 40:1-3 below, how can you see God's rescue of you helping others?**

    "I waited patiently for the LORD; He turned to me and heard my cry. He lifted me out of the slimy pit, out of the mud and mire; He set my feet on a rock and gave me a firm place to stand. He put a new song in my mouth, a hymn of praise to our God. Many will see and fear and put their trust in the LORD."

What joy to know that nothing was wasted and that lives will be touched and souls saved. In the end, every drop of heartache will be replaced with unending joy.

I love the story in Judges 7 about the little army of 300 led by Gideon. Each man, armed with a sword, and pots covering torches, set out to fight an army more numerous than sand on the seashore. Once in position, they smashed the pots. The broken vessels fell away revealing the torches of light that sent the enemy fleeing (Judges 7:15-21). In the same way, your broken pieces can be used to reveal the healing light of Christ.

God shared a beautiful truth with Daniel about the end times, "Those who have insight will shine brightly like the brightness of the expanse of heaven, and those who lead the many to righteousness, like the stars forever and ever" (Daniel 12:3 NASB).

Regardless of how young or old, we can shine the light of Christ.

With God all things are possible (Matthew 19:26). With Jesus in our lives, He not only gives us the ability for eternal life, but the ability to overcome.

- **Read Revelation 12:11[74], how did they overcome the devil?**

- **Read again Isaiah 43:18-19. What is God doing now?**

"The Lord says, 'Forget what happened before, and do not think about the past. Look at the new thing I am going to do. It is already happening. Don't you see it? I will make a road in the desert and rivers in the dry land" (Isaiah 43:18-19 NCV).

- **Read Philippians 3:13-14[75]. What should you do and what will you receive when you do?**

> *"Let the past sleep, but let it sleep on the bosom of Christ, and go out into the irresistible future with him." ~ Oswald Chambers*

When the devil throws stink bombs, God blows back the stink to restore, renew, and use everything for good. When we allow God to walk us through and provide soul healing, He uses our difficulties to help in the battle for others.

What better way to defeat the enemy than by turning the evil used against us to provide freedom for others? All around us, people are dying – mentally, physically, and spiritually, and our stories may well be part of their rescue.

What the devil used to hurt you, throw back on him, heap the mess right back on his slimy head by allowing God to heal you.

> *"We need you — It is the wounded ones who makes us heal and the hurting ones who make us honest and it is the broken ones who put us back together again and it is the scarred ones who make the Body of Christ sensitive." ~ Ann Voskamp*[76]

When God prompts you, be willing to share your testimony. Don't hide what God has done in your life. Don't let the pain the enemy caused you to be wasted. Allow God's healing, allow His light to shine on you, and in you, and through you.

Pray with me?

Heavenly Father, You know my scars. You know the difficulties of my journey. Oh God, heal and restore me. Shine Your healing light on my wounded soul, and then may Your light shine from within me to help heal and set others free.

I ask these things in the name of Jesus Christ, who is my Savior. Amen.

- **Would you take a moment and pray? Whatever scars you have, take them to God. Take them and allow His healing. Let His light shine on your wounds so His glory can heal you and shine His light through you.**

"If you only look at us, you might well miss the brightness. We carry this precious Message around in the unadorned clay pots of our ordinary lives. That's to prevent anyone from confusing God's incomparable power with us. As it is, there's not much chance of that. You know for yourselves that we're not much to look at. We've been surrounded and battered by troubles, but we're not demoralized; we're not sure what to do, but we know that God knows what to do; we've been spiritually terrorized, but God hasn't left our side; we've been thrown down, but we haven't broken. ...We're not keeping this quiet, not on your life. Just like the psalmist who wrote, 'I believed it, so I said it,' we say what we believe. And what we believe is that the One who raised up the Master Jesus will just as certainly raise us up with you, alive. Every detail works to your advantage and to God's glory: more and more grace, more and more people, more and more praise!

"So, we're not giving up. How could we! Even though on the outside it often looks like things are falling apart on us, **on the inside, where God is making new life, not a day goes by without his unfolding grace.** These hard times are small potatoes compared to the coming good times, the lavish celebration prepared for us. There's far more here than meets the eye. The things we see now are here today, gone tomorrow. But the things we can't see now will last forever" (2 Corinthians 4:10-18 MSG).

"**Let your light so shine** before men, that they may see your good works and glorify your Father in heaven. Here's another way to put it: You're here to be light, bringing out the God-colors in the world. God is not a secret to be kept. We're going public with this, as public as a city on a hill. If I make you light-bearers, you don't think I'm going to hide you under a bucket, do you? I'm putting you on a light stand. Now that I've put you there on a hilltop, on a light stand—**shine!**"

"...you are a chosen race, a royal priesthood, a holy nation, a people for God's own possession, so that you may **proclaim the excellencies of Him who has called you out of darkness into His marvelous light**. ...walk in a manner worthy of the Lord, to please Him in all respects, bearing fruit in every good work and increasing in the knowledge of God; strengthened with all power, according to His glorious might, for the attaining of all steadfastness and patience; joyously giving thanks to the Father, who has qualified us to share in the inheritance of the **saints in Light**" (Matthew 5:16 NKJV, Matthew 5:14-15 MSG, 1 Peter 2:9 NASB, Colossians 1:10-12 NASB).

Session Three

Head rest

Anyone else have head battles? You know, battles that take place in your head? If someone gave out trophies for this non-sport, I would have a shelf full.

I've had my brain whirling with possible scenarios; if "this" thing happened, how would I respond, what would I need to do and say. If "that" thing happened, how would I respond, what would I need to do and say. The more I analyzed and worried, the less prepared I felt for what might actually happen.

Satan tries to get us to imagine possible scenarios, because the more we put ourselves in an imaginary situation, the more worked-up we will be if that situation happens. If we think someone will be hostile, and we go in with a hostile attitude we may cause the other person to react in a hostile manner.

The devil twists and manipulates to get us to think negatively about anything and everyone.

Too many times I'll look at a situation, hear about a situation, be involved in a situation, and then get in my head and play out different scenarios as I search for answers and solutions.

Sometimes I'll wake up in the middle of the night thinking about an uncomfortable conversation that needs to happen, or someone who is going through a difficult time, or politics, or the world's problems, or a million other issues, and I'll battle in my head on what to say, how to fix something, or what another person should do or say, and on and on it goes until I've beaten myself bloody without talking to anyone but myself or solving any problems.

Ack!

My little head makes no headway unless I run to God who has all wisdom, knowledge, and understanding.

> *"When we talk to ourselves, we're not talking to anyone very smart, because our outlook is very limited. But if we talk to God, we're talking to someone who knows everything. He knows what he promised in the beginning, and he knows exactly how to fulfill those promises no matter the circumstances." ~ Jim Cymbala*[77]

The devil's darts comes in various methods, and he knows how to attack our thoughts. He wants us exhausted physically, mentally, and spiritually. Mind games with the enemy are not games. The devil is out to capture our thoughts so he can keep us captive in our thoughts. Fortunately, we don't have to play mind games with the enemy.

So, how do you get out of the battlefield of the brain? The bombardment of thoughts will come, but you have a choice what is allowed to stay. There are rules of engagement in battles.

- **What does James share in James 4:7?**[78]

- **What does 2 Corinthians 10:3-5[79] say you can do with your thoughts? What are your weapons?**

James tells us to resist the devil and he will flee and Paul reminds us to take every thought captive to the obedience of Christ.

- **Based on 1 Corinthians 2:16[80], what else are you given?**

When Christ is in you, you have His power to free you. Plus, you are additionally blessed... "For God did not give us a spirit of timidity or cowardice or fear, but [**He has given us a spirit] of power and of love and of sound judgment** and personal discipline [**abilities that result in a calm, well-balanced mind and self-control**]" (2 Timothy 1:7 AMP).

The freedom given by Jesus Christ is for **every** aspect of your life. When thoughts come, when the head battles start battling, remember the power you are given in Christ, remember you are given sound judgement and a calm and well-balanced mind.

Take every thought captive, check them by shining God's light and throw out any not in line with His truth.

You can control your thoughts in a fashion similar to an air-traffic controller. The thoughts may fly around, but you decide which ones have permission to land.

I'm still learning this skill, and I am amazed at the benefits of being aware of thoughts and filtering out the ones that have no benefit for my soul and well-being.

- **According to Philippians 4:6-7[81] how do we control our anxious thoughts? What happens when we do this?**

God never leaves you defenseless. Even with real and worrisome concerns, you can bring them to your loving and caring God. As you bring your concerns in prayer and thanksgiving, the sentinel of God's peace and truth stands guard over your heart and mind.

As God's child, you have a right (and the power) to deny access to thoughts that waste time, that would cause you to stumble or pull you away from God, or those that deprive you of sleep and soul rest.

Taking thoughts captive isn't just about shoving them behind bars; it is exploring God's truth and finding the reality of God's might, power, forgiveness, mercy, and grace. Freedom comes from, and in, God's truth.

Knowing God's word demolishes the lies of the enemy and helps corral unruly thoughts.

Paul tells us in Ephesians 6:17 that the Word of God is the Sword of the Spirit. Hebrews 4:12 tells us "the word of God is living and active and sharper than any two-edged sword and piercing as far as the division of soul and spirit, of both joints and marrow, and able to judge the thoughts and intentions of the heart."

Take every thought captive, wrap it in God's truth, throw it out, smash it, destroy it, and live free. For, greater is our God than the one who is in the world.

Wield your sword of the Spirit, and smash, demolish, and force lies and bad thoughts to succumb to the power of our Most High God and mighty Savior. God's Word, truth, is your offensive weapon, your sword. No matter what your concerns, worries, or thoughts, you can find truth in Who God is to help you stand firm in the heat of life's battles. Whatever is faced, you can find your needs met and your soul-rest in the truth of God's Word.

- **May I also suggest a mental checklist to control thoughts? When a thought comes to mind, ask yourself the following questions...**

    Does this thought honor God?

    Will this thought be pleasing to God? (See Psalm 104:34[82])

    Will thinking about this thought solve or help anything or anyone?

    Will contemplating this thought bring me peace or rest?

    What does God's Word tell me about a thought like this?

- **Write down additional questions and truths to help in your thought battle.**

Unfortunately, I have had times I wasn't satisfied with God's way, and I've traveled down the wrong roads.

I ignored warning signs and headed over the cliff of temptation. I didn't just step my toes in the mud, I went headfirst, and wallowed in the pigsty of sin.

Sin collisions always results in wreckage, and out of the debris crawls regret, guilt, and condemnation. Satan, instigator, and deceiver, sets us up to fall, or sets us up for abuse and misuse, then stands by with virtual camera in hand to capture images. He whispers, shouts, and screams our failures or blames us for what he started in the first place. The enemy is right there to rub our noses in the mess and blackmail us into ineffectiveness in Christ's kingdom.

- **What visual is given in 1 Peter 5:8[83] of the devil?**

- **Based on John 10:10[84], what is the devil's mission?**

Satan is the father of lies (John 8:44), he is out to steal, kill, and destroy, and is a roaring lion seeking to devour. Jesus came to give life in abundant. God's Word, the sword of the Spirit, cuts off the devil's lies and his power.

Next time the devil comes to call, remind him there is nothing in your past that hasn't been forgiven, restored, and redeemed by the grace of Jesus Christ.

God grants weapons, gives a battle plan, warns of demonic attacks, and shows how to defend yourself. You don't have to live in the stench; there are methods for stink removal.

You have a choice as to whether past wounds are medals for the enemy or medals for Christ's healing and restoration.

- **What promise is given in Isaiah 43:18-19?**[85]

God blesses with new mercies and opportunities. His mercies are new *every* morning. What's done is done, but what is to come through our Savior, is new, vibrant, and exciting. Jesus—the way, the truth, and the life, Prince of Peace, Lord of Lords—rescues from sin, the pain of yesterday, and gives hope for tomorrow.

- **Based on what Jesus said in John 8:31-32,**[86] **what happens when we hold to His teaching?**

- **What promise did Jesus give His followers in Luke 21:15?**[87]

When you hold to the teaching of Jesus, when you really are His disciples, then you'll know the truth, and The Truth will set you free. God also gives words and wisdom which no opponent will be able to resist or refute.

> *"Freedom from spiritual conflicts and bondage is not a power encounter; it's a truth encounter. Satan is a deceiver, and he will work undercover at all costs. But the truth of God's Word exposes him and his lies."*
> ~ Neil T. Anderson[88]

During spiritual warfare I had a tendency to pray in my mind, asking God for protection, guidance, wisdom, and help.

Unfortunately, I still felt rather bloodied by the enemy.

One night while under spiritual attack, I prayed in my mind for God for help, even recounting the promises God has given, but still made no headway in the battle.

Then, I felt within my spirit an urge to recite God's promises and His word out loud. At first, I hesitated and wondered why that was necessary. But then, I realized by speaking out loud, I released God's truth into the air, and God's truth sets us free. By merely praying and rebuking the devil in my head, I had kept my sword of the Spirit in the sheath.

How did Jesus resist the devil? When Jesus was confronted by Satan in the wilderness, Jesus quoted scripture (see Matthew 4). There is power in the word of God and power when we speak God's word. Rebuking the enemy comes with speaking God's word.

We can whimper and cry all day at the enemy, we can even shout at the devil, but when we quote scripture as Jesus did, that is when we use God's power, that is when the devil will flee, and that is when we can stand firm.

Behind every fear, worry and anxiety, is a demonic lie. Satan wants you to believe in the midst of your problems, in the middle of storms, in any trouble you face, God is not sufficient, not powerful enough, not loving enough, and unable or unwilling to help. The Truth is God is loving, ALL-powerful, ALL-sufficient, just and righteous, loving, and He always takes care of His children.

The battle is not with flesh and blood. Behind all the mess of the world is Satan. Fortunately, God blesses with weapons.

- **Read the following verses in Ephesians and highlight and note the weapons you are given to battle against the devil.**

•

> "Put on God's whole armor [the armor of a heavy-armed soldier which God supplies], that you may be able successfully to stand up against [all] the strategies and the deceits of the devil. For we are not wrestling with flesh and blood [contending only with physical opponents], but against the despotisms, against the powers, against [the master spirits who are] the world rulers of this present darkness, against the spirit forces of wickedness in the heavenly (supernatural) sphere. Therefore, put on God's complete armor, that you may be able to resist and stand your ground on the evil day [of danger], and, having done all [the crisis demands], to stand [firmly in your place]. Stand therefore [hold your ground], having tightened the belt of truth around your loins and having put on the breastplate of integrity and of moral rectitude and right standing with God, and having shod your feet in preparation [to face the enemy with the firm-footed stability, the promptness, and the readiness produced by the good news] of the Gospel of peace. Lift up over all the [covering] shield of saving faith, upon which you can quench all the flaming missiles of the wicked [one]. And take the helmet of salvation and the sword that the Spirit wields, which is the Word of God" (Ephesians 6:11-17 AMPC).

When the enemy assaults you with lies, ask the Holy Spirit to reveal God's truth. Go to God, ask Him to show you the lie behind the enemy attack, then combat that lie with God's truth.

Remember who God is, remember His promises and remember and know His Word.

During battles, go to God and ask Him, **"What is the lie the enemy has planted?"**

Pray with me?

Heavenly Father, please show me the lie behind this battle, insecurity, frustration, fear, worry, _____
_____

God please reveal **Your** truth so I may stand firm on Your truth and combat every enemy lie.

God please help me to find scriptures to pray about each situation. Open my eyes to see beyond the person, situation, or circumstance that seems to be causing the problem(s).

Heavenly Father, show me the lie the devil has planted and then help me to remember Your truth and quiet me with Your love. There is nothing too hard for You, nothing is impossible for You, for You are ALL-mighty and forever loving. You will never leave me or forsake me. Thank You, Father, that in Your light and truth, every enemy will fall.

I ask these things in the name of Your Son, Jesus Christ, who is my Savior. Amen.

On the next few pages, I've listed some of the lies the devil puts in our thoughts. Using scripture, I've countered with prayer using The Truth in God's Word

- **Underline, highlight, make note, and pray the truths you need in the scenarios below and on the next pages.**

The enemy lies, you shouldn't have been born.
Pray God's truth. God, You saved me, You formed me in my mother's body. You have made everything stretching out the skies and spreading out the earth. Before You made me in my mother's womb, You chose me. Thank You, Father! Before I was born, You set me apart for a special work. You know the plans You have for me. You have good plans, not plans to hurt me but to give me a hope and a good future. Thank you, God! (Isaiah 44:24, Jeremiah 1:5, Jeremiah 29:11).

The enemy lies, no one loves or wants you.
Pray God's truth. God, thank You that You love me with an everlasting love. You have drawn me to Yourself with Your loving-kindness. Jesus said, as the Father loved me, so have I loved you. I am loved! For as high as the heavens are above the earth, so great is Your steadfast love toward those who fear You. Long before You laid down earth's foundations, You had me in mind, and settled as the focus of Your love, to be made whole and holy by Your love. Long, long ago You decided to adopt me into Your family through Jesus Christ. (What pleasure You took in planning this!). You wanted me to enter into the celebration of Your lavish gift-giving by the hand of Your beloved Son. It's in Christ that I find out who I am and what I are living for. Long before I first heard of Christ and got my hopes up, God had His eye on me, had designs on me for glorious living, part of the overall purpose He is working out in everything and everyone (Jeremiah 31:3, John 15:9, Psalm 103:11, Ephesians 1:3-6 MSG, Ephesians 11-12 MSG).

The enemy lies, you are alone.
Pray God's truth. I will not be afraid or discouraged, for the Lord will personally go ahead of me. He will be with me; He will neither fail me nor abandon me. God said, "don't be afraid, for I am with you. Don't be discouraged, for I am your God." He will strengthen me and help me. He will hold me up with His

victorious right hand. When I pass through the waters, He will be with me; and through the rivers, they shall not overwhelm me; when I walk through fire I shall not be burned, and the flame shall not consume me. For the Lord my God is living among me. He is a mighty Savior. He will take delight in me with gladness. With His love, He will calm all my fears. He will rejoice over me with joyful songs (Deuteronomy 31:8 NLT, Isaiah 41:10 NLT, Isaiah 43:2 ESV, Zephaniah 3:17 NLT).

The enemy lies, you've gone too far from God's grace.
Pray God's Truth... The LORD's power is enough to save me. He can hear me when I ask Him for help. God's mercy is great, and He loves me very much. Though I was spiritually dead because of the things I did against God, He gave me new life with Christ. I have been saved by God's grace. And He raised me up with Christ and gave me a seat with Him in the heavens. He did this for those in Christ Jesus so that for all future time He could show the very great riches of His grace by being kind to me in Christ Jesus. I have been saved by grace through believing. I did not save myself; it was a gift from God. God rescued me from dead-end alleys and dark dungeons. He's set me up in the kingdom of the Son He loves me so much, the Son who got me out of the pit I was in, got rid of the sins I was doomed to keep repeating (Isaiah 59:1 NCV, Ephesians 2:4-8 NCV, Colossians 1:13-14 MSG).

The enemy lies, no one understands.
Pray God's truth. God You know when I sit down and when I get up. You know my thoughts before I think them. He has compassion on me. He knows how I was formed and remembers I am but dust. He knows, understands, and knows me (Psalm 139:2, Psalm 103:13-14, Jeremiah 9:24).

The enemy lies, there is no hope or help.
Pray God's truth. My help comes from the LORD, the Maker

of heaven and earth. He will not let my foot slip. He who watches over me will not slumber. He's my shade at my right hand. The sun won't harm me by day, nor the moon by night. The Lord will keep me from all harm. He will watch over my life. He'll watch over my coming and going now and forever. The Lord is my help and my shield. Find rest my soul, in God alone. My hope comes from Him (Psalm 33:20, Psalm 62:5, Psalm 121).

The enemy lies, you are unprotected.
Pray God's truth. The name of the LORD is a strong tower, the righteous run to it and are safe. He is my hiding place. He will protect me from trouble and surround me with songs of deliverance. The Lord is faithful, and He will strengthen and protect me from the evil one. He will cover me with His feathers, and under His wings I will find refuge; His faithfulness will be my shield and rampart. He is my rock, fortress and deliverer. God is my rock, in whom I take refuge. He is my shield and stronghold (Proverbs 18:10, Psalm 32:7, 2 Thessalonians 3:3, Psalm 91:4, Psalm 18:2).

The God-given truth is, you are loved and were formed and created by the God of the universe. In Christ, you are forgiven and free from condemnation, and are redeemed, restored, renewed, complete, and loved forever, and that's the God-given truth!

Pray with me?

Heavenly Father, I praise You and thank You for who You are.

Your love reaches above the heavens. Your mercies are new every morning. Regardless of what I face, regardless of what has happened in the past, regardless of what will happen in the future, You are in control and You are just, righteous, and merciful.

God, reveal the enemy lies that keep me in bondage. Help me to live in Your Truth, to walk in Your Way, and to live freely in Your Life.

Free me Lord, to be used freely for You!

Overwhelming

"Please listen and answer me, for I am overwhelmed by my troubles. From the ends of the earth, I cry to you for help when my heart is overwhelmed. Lead me to the towering rock of safety, for you are my safe refuge, a fortress where my enemies cannot reach me" (Psalm 61:2-3, Psalm 55:2 NLT).

Sobbing, I struggled to breathe. News of a loved one falling away from God left me reeling and staggering with sorrow. Other family members health continued to decline, and prayer needs from family, friends, and the crazy state of the world, overwhelmed my thoughts and soul.

My desperate prayers pounded on heaven's door for help, healing, and salvation for my loved ones. Unless God intervened, nothing would change, nothing would be fixed, and no one would be saved. Looking for a way to cope, tears flowed as I banged my fists against the wall. The devil had again attacked my family and left pieces of my heart scattered on the ground.

Overcome with sorrow, God's still small voice spoke into my soul – "***You've forgotten who I am***."

Ouch.

God's right. He knows my anxiety, worries, and concerns were overwhelming because I had forgotten the power and might of my all-powerful, all-mighty God.

The Israelites struggled with this for generations. They were rescued in miraculous ways from slavery, and with God's help destroyed nations bigger than they were. God provided in amazing ways for their every need. But then they would forget, and they would wander away and life always got very difficult. When they would turn back to God, He would again rescue and help.

The Israelites were in Egypt over 400 years and spent much of that time in captivity. The Bible doesn't share much about the captive years, but sure does tell about God's amazing rescue.

I wonder sometimes if we spend so much time processing our time in captivity that we fail to see God's rescue. His deliverance is often missed or dismissed because the focus is on the timing or how we thought the rescue would come. Then all the ways God worked (and is working) was or is completely missed.

Now personally I prefer a rescue before a bad thing happens -- like the damsel in distress who is rescued by the knight in shining armor.

Uh, but then I remember the damsel *was* in distress.

Bummer. I guess rescues don't take place unless one is needed.

Fortunately, God promises to get us through, and not just through, but safely home with Him. God's rescues take place with the back against the Red Sea, in the lion's den, and in the fiery furnace.

And oh, how God's rescues take place in the quiet moments of grief, in the desperate moments of pain, and in the tender moments of healing.

Rescue will come. God's rescue will always come. God's rescues come in various forms – sometimes through blocking an attack, sometimes through healing, sometimes through various methods that we prefer, but God's rescues also come by bringing someone safely into His presence.

Jesus said He came to set the captives free, and when He sets us free, we will indeed be free.[89] Freedom in Christ is freedom from sin (talk about a wonderful rescue!), freedom with new life, and freedom for eternity. Our minds, our souls, need to remember, need to be fed with the truth of the amazing power of our amazing God.

- **How did God rescue the Israelites in Exodus 14:13-30?**[90]

- **How did God help the Israelites in Joshua 3:15-17?**[91]

- **How did God help the Israelites defeat Jericho in Joshua 6?**[92]

- **What did Jesus tell us in Matthew 19:26?**[93]

God's power is **big** enough to help you cross over any concern or problem, He will part the way before you and help you step over and through the ruins to victory against any enemy. All things are possible with God and nothing is impossible for God.

- **According to Daniel 3, what happened when Shadrach, Meshach, and Abednego were thrown in the fiery furnace? (See Daniel 3:21-24)**[94]

The three young men were not spared being thrown into the fire yet were given the amazing privilege of walking through the fire with God. And when they exited the fire, they didn't even smell like smoke.

In the midst of overwhelming difficulties, your freedom is found in the overwhelming truth of the might, power, and love of God.

- **Using the Amplified version of Isaiah 26:3-4, underline what God will do and who God is.**

> "You will keep in perfect and constant peace the one whose mind is steadfast [that is, committed and focused on You—in both inclination and character], because he trusts and takes refuge in You [with hope and confident expectation]. Trust [confidently] in the Lord forever [He is your fortress, your shield, your banner], for the Lord God is an everlasting Rock [the Rock of Ages]."

Oh, if we truly understood the depth of the love of God. If we really knew and could comprehend that we are completely and totally loved, wouldn't we be fearless?

- **Read Ephesians 3:17-19[95]. What are you rooted and grounded in? What do you need to comprehend or grasp? What are you filled with?**

As Christians we are rooted in love, in the breadth, length, height, and depth of the love of Christ and filled with the fullness of God. And therefore, according to Romans 8:38-39, nothing "neither death, nor life, nor angels, nor principalities, nor things present, nor things to come, nor powers, nor height, nor depth, nor any other created thing, will be able to separate us from the love of God, which is in Christ Jesus our Lord." Read those truths again. Can you just shout hallelujah!

No power is bigger than God's power.

No love is bigger than God's love.

Nothing and no one can separate you from God's love, and nothing and no one can snatch you from the safety of His loving hands.

- **Read the verses below and allow God's truth to wash over you. Highlight and if possible read the verses aloud.**

    "So, do not fear, for I am with you; do not be dismayed, for I am your God. I will strengthen you and help you; I will uphold you with my righteous right hand" (Isaiah 41:10 NIV).

    "For I am the Lord your God, who upholds your right hand, who says to you, 'Do not fear, I will help you'" (Isaiah 41:13 NASB).

"If the Lord had not been on our side when people attacked us, they would have swallowed us alive when their anger flared against us; the flood would have engulfed us, the torrent would have swept over us, the raging waters would have swept us away. Praise be to the Lord, who has not let us be torn by their teeth. We have escaped like a bird from the fowler's snare; the snare has been broken, and we have escaped. Our help is in the name of the Lord, the Maker of heaven and earth" (Psalm 124:2-8 NIV).

"Then they cried out to the Lord in their trouble, and he brought them out of their distress. He stilled the storm to a whisper; the waves of the sea were hushed. They were glad when it grew calm, and he guided them to their desired haven" (Psalm 107:28-30 NIV).

"O Lord God of hosts, who is mighty like You, O Lord? Your faithfulness also surrounds You. You rule the raging of the sea; when its waves rise, You still them" (Psalm 89:8-9 NKJV).

"You answer us with awesome and righteous deeds, God our Savior, the hope of all the ends of the earth and of the farthest seas, who formed the mountains by your power, having armed yourself with strength, who stilled the roaring of the seas, the roaring of their waves, and the turmoil of the nations. The whole earth is filled with awe at your wonders; where morning dawns, where evening fades, you call forth songs of joy" (Psalm 65:5-8 NIV).

Remember who God is and remember who you are in Christ. Remember what God has done, and Who has power over all. Remember. Remember nothing is impossible for God.

In overwhelming times, turn the focus off the problems and back on the Savior.

Oh, that we would be like those who saw Jesus and were overwhelmed with awe. **"When the crowd saw Jesus, they were overwhelmed with awe**, and they ran to greet him" (Mark 9:15 NLT).

Overwhelmed by the depth, height, breadth, and width of the love of our Savior, we find confident, undaunted courage and peace in His loving, overcoming, conquering power.

Happy sigh...

> *"If we are obsessed by God, nothing else can get into our lives-- not concerns, nor tribulations, nor worries. And now we understand why our Lord so emphasized the sin of worrying. How can we dare to be so absolutely unbelieving when God totally surrounds us? To be obsessed by God is to have an effective barricade against all the assaults of the enemy."*
> *~ Oswald Chambers*[96]

God, I have been overwhelmed by trouble; overwhelmed by things in my life and things happening in the world. Help me to turn my focus on You and remember that You are still in control, You are always in control.

Help me to be so overwhelmed by Your great love that I'm not overwhelmed by anything else.

Resting in trials

A successful attorney in Chicago, Horatio Spafford was active in church and blessed with a wife and four daughters. A series of misfortunes began when the great Chicago fire of 1871 wiped out his family's extensive real estate investments. Even through the difficulties, Spafford held firm to his belief and faith in God.

Horatio was a friend and supporter of the great evangelist D.L. Moody. When Moody began a campaign in Great Britain, Spafford planned to join them to assist. Seeing this as a wonderful opportunity for the whole family, passage was booked on the S.S. Ville du Harve in November of 1873.

Before he could leave, Horatio was detained by urgent business. He sent his family ahead and planned to join them as soon as possible.

Unfortunately, the ship carrying his wife and daughters was struck by an English vessel and sank in twelve minutes. Two hundred and twenty-six people drowned, including his four daughters. Only his wife miraculously survived.

Heartbroken, Spafford boarded another ship to meet his bereaved wife. Upon reaching the approximate sight of the shipwreck, he stood on the deck of his ship.

Sensing God's presence and unexplained peace, he wrote these words. "When peace like a river, attendeth my way, when sorrows like sea billows roll—whatever my lot, Thou hast taught me to say, it is well with my soul."

How can one write, "It is well with my soul" when tragedy has just struck? Only through God. Only God can make us well with our soul in the midst of tragedy and turmoil.

Peace is found through a soul perspective, looking beyond today to the forever. When God is our focus, our direction, and our love, there is nothing on earth that can shake or remove our eternal stability.

- **Write Isaiah 41:10[97]. It is well with my soul because God promised...**

- **Highlight the promises in Psalm 18:2. It is well with my soul because...**" The Lord is my rock, my fortress, and my Savior; my God is my rock, in whom I find protection. He is my shield, the power that saves me, and my place of safety."

- **Write Isaiah 26:3[98]. It is well with my soul because...**

- **Write Psalm 27:5[99]. It is well with my soul because**

- **Highlight the promises in Isaiah 43:2-3. It is well with my soul because ....** "When you pass through the waters, I will be with you; and through the rivers, they shall not overflow you. When you walk through the fire, you shall not be burned, nor shall the flame scorch you. For I am the Lord your God, the Holy One of Israel, your Savior...".

- **Write Psalm 4:8[100]. It is well with my soul because...**

- **Underline Proverbs 18:10. It is well with my soul because....** "The name of the Lord is a strong tower; the righteous runs into it and is safe."

- **Write Isaiah 54:5[101]. It is well with my soul because...**

- **Underline the promises. It is well with my soul because God promised...** "Even when you are old, I will take care of you, even when you have gray hair, I will carry you. I made you and I will support you; I will carry you and rescue you" (Isaiah 46:4 NET).

- **Write John 16:33[102]. It is well with my soul because Jesus said and promised...**

God says, "Do not fear," and thankfully He doesn't stop there, He reassures, "for I am with you" (Isaiah 41:10, Isaiah 43:5).

Frightening things exist in this world, but God is with you in the world. Through the difficulties, through the trials, God's love is unfailing. He won't leave or forsake you.

God understands your frailties. When your flesh wobbles with worry, God's comfort flows through. His strong arms catch and surround you, and He will guide through the light and through the dark.

As a good Father steadies His young child who is trying to walk, God holds you tight and will steady you through the hard times.

> *"Trials are not 'chastisement'. No earthly father goes on chastising a loving child. That is a common thought about suffering, but I am quite sure it is a wrong thought. Paul's suffering were not that, nor are yours. They are battle wounds. They are signs of high confidence—honours. The Father holds His children very close to His heart when they are going through such rough places as this." ~ Amy Carmichael* [103]

Peter reminds us, "...trials will show that your faith is genuine. It is being tested as fire tests and purifies gold—though your faith is far more precious than mere gold. So, when your faith remains strong through many trials, it will bring you much praise and glory and honor on the day when Jesus Christ is revealed to the whole world" (1 Peter 1:7 NLT).

No matter what you face, glory will come. God is the deliverer, healer, restorer, and redeemer.

If illness attacks you, enemies surround you, difficulties assail you, there is nothing too big, nothing impossible, nothing beyond the reach of our all-powerful, loving God. Don't be afraid for He is with you, and He will be with you. Praise God, The Great I AM is with you!

God is with you from beginning to the end and covers you from beginning to the end. God was with you, is with you, and will be with you.

"I am the Alpha and the Omega, the Beginning and the End, says the Lord, who is and who was and who is to come, the Almighty" (Revelation 1:8). The A-to-Z of God covers your every A-to-Z of needs.

I often go through the alphabet to remember the qualities of God during times of difficulties, when I'm trying to get to sleep, or just wanting/needing to remember the power and wonder of God. On the next few pages is my list.

- **As you read through, note, underline or highlight the comforting truths of who God is in the situation(s) you are facing.**

God is the **A**lpha and Omega, **A**donai, **A**lmighty (ALL-mighty), **A**ll-powerful, the **A**ncient of days, **A**lways-present, **A**wesome and **A**ble to save.
God is **B**eautiful, the **B**uilder of everything, who is my **B**anner.
God is the **C**reator of heaven and earth, **C**ompassionate, God of all **C**omfort.
God is **D**efender and **D**eliverer.
God is **E**ternal, **E**ver-present, **E**verlasting, **E**l Shaddai (Lord God Almighty), **E**l Elyon (The Most High God), **E**lohim.
God is a **F**aithful, **F**orgiving, **F**ather.
God is **G**reat and **G**ood, and **G**racious.

God is **H**oly, **H**igh and lifted up, **H**ope, **H**ealer, the Lord of **H**osts.

God is **I** Am.

God is **J**ehovah **J**ireh (The Lord Will Provide), **J**oy and a **J**ust **J**udge.

God is **K**ing and is **K**ind.

God is **L**oving **L**ord of all, **L**ord our God.

God is **M**ighty, the **M**ost High, **M**aker, and **M**arvelous.

God is **N**ame above all names, Jehovah **N**issi (The Lord my banner), the God over all **N**ations.

God is **O**mnipotent, **O**mniscient, **O**nly true God.

God is **P**owerful, the **P**otter, my **P**eace.

God **Q**uiets us with His love.

God is **R**ighteous, my **R**ock, my **R**edeemer, El **R**oi (the God who sees me), Jehovah-**R**aah (The Lord My Shepherd), Jehovah **R**apha (The Lord That Heals)

God is **S**trong, **S**avior, **S**hepherd, **S**overeign Lord, **S**hield, **S**alvation, Jehovah **S**halom (The Lord Is Peace), Jehovah **S**abaoth (The Lord of Hosts).

God is **T**rue, **T**riumphant, **T**ruth, and **T**imeless.

God is **U**nfailing, **U**pright, with all **U**nderstanding.

God is **V**ictorious.

God is **W**onderful, **W**ise and **W**orthy of all **W**orship.

God is e**X**alted and e**X**traordinary.

God is **Y**ahweh.

God is God of **Z**ion who is **Z**ealous for his people.

- **What descriptions of our wonderful God can you add to the list?**

> *"God is above all things, beneath all things, outside of all things, and inside of all things. God is above, but He's not pushed up. He's beneath, but He's not pressed down. He's outside, but He's not excluded. He's inside, but He's not confined. God is above all things presiding, beneath all things sustaining, outside of all things embracing and inside of all things filling." ~ A. W. Tozer[104]*

- **What did Jesus tell the Samaritan woman in John 4:10?[105]**

Jesus told the woman, "if you knew the gift of God." The more we know about God, the more we understand and grasp who God is, the depth and height of God's love for us, the firmer we can stand during trials.

In Hosea 4:6, God says His people are destroyed from lack of knowledge. Don't let anyone or anything destroy the knowledge of how much God loves you.

Read God's word, remember God's word, and live in the truth of God's word.

What if you knew how much you are loved? What if you really, really, really believed God loved you? Would you see God, yourself, your life, and others differently? Would you believe that, know that, live that, remember that all things work for the good because your heavenly Father loves you, really, really, really loves you?

What if you knew how much you are loved? Would you stop beating up yourself for your mistakes?

Would you forgive yourself and others so that you can live free in the forgiveness of God, trusting Him to make you right, to make all things right?

What if you knew how much you are loved? Would you give God your regrets, your sins, your wayward ways, remembering God is the Father waiting with love for the prodigal to return home? Would you remember that nothing can separate you from God's love?

What if you knew how much you are loved? Would you move forward with excitement because you know you are loved?

Would you stop looking back and instead look up, would you trust that God loves you enough, loves you so much, that His love covers your past, present, and future?

What if you knew how much you are loved? Would you remember God is the Father who sent His Son to earth for your rescue? Would you remember Jesus came willingly for you, to save you, to free you, to give you an eternal hope-filled, joyful home? Would you, could you, will you relax and rest in God's love?

What if you knew how much you are loved? Would you remember you have the power of God living within you to help you through whatever you have gone through and whatever you face in the future?

What if *I* lived believing and knowing I am loved? God's love is unfailing and everlasting because God's love is not just an emotion, God is love. What if I allowed God's love to wash over me, filling me, restoring me, mending me, cleansing me, and setting me free forever?

God's Spirit whispers...

If you knew Me, you wouldn't be worried.
If you knew Me, you would know My heart is always good.
If you knew Me, you would trust Me.
If you knew Me, you would not be afraid.
If you knew Me, you would know you can always believe Me.
If you knew Me, you wouldn't believe that lie.
If you knew Me, you would know My plans for you are always good.
If you knew Me, you would know I will never leave you or forsake you.
If you knew Me, you would rest.
If you knew Me, you would know I will be with you forever, and ever.
If you knew Me, you would never doubt My love.
If you knew Me, you would know My love is unfailing.
Know, and always remember, how much I love you.

---- your loving God.

What if *I* knew, really knew how much I am loved? Oh Father, I believe, help my unbelief. Help me to know You, for You are love. Thank You God for Your amazing love. Let me swim, diving deep into the beauty of Your unfailing, everlasting kindness and love. Help me to know, and always remember, how much I am loved.

"I have loved you with an everlasting love. For the Lord is good; His lovingkindness is everlasting and His faithfulness to all generations" (Jeremiah 31:3, Psalm 100:5 NASB).

"Things which eye has not seen and ear has not heard, and which have not entered the heart of man, all that God has prepared for those who love Him. For I am convinced that neither death, nor life, nor angels, nor principalities, nor things present, nor things to come, nor powers, nor height, nor depth, nor any other created thing, will be able to separate us from the love of God, which is in Christ Jesus our Lord. For God is love" (1 Corinthians 2:9, Romans 8:38-39, 1 John 4:16 NASB).

> *"You must seek God's gift of peace right where you are because that is where God's peace always is ... right where you are. We are often tempted to look in remote places and circumstances for the gift of peace, especially when suffering from the pain of loss. It is necessary and productive for you to see the gift of God's peace is given to you where you are, when you are ready for it, when you want it, when you surrender your will and your life into the care and keeping of God. Then, it happens."*
> *~ Paul F. Keller*

Resting in the wait

For years I prayed and waited for healing. I've prayed and waited for answers to problems that didn't seem to have solutions.

My life has been stuck in many holding patterns, and there are times I've been so restless I thought I would burst out of my skin.

I'm still waiting for some things, some promises I believe the Lord has made, and continue to wait for many prayers to be answered.

Life waits come through illness, life changes, and life challenges. Waiting is difficult. Not fun. Taxing. And yet, **and yet**, God promises in Isaiah 40:31 that **those who wait on the Lord will renew their strength, mount up with wings like eagles, run and not be weary, walk and not faint**.

My sweet friend, Teena Goble, filled me in on some wonderful truths about the verse in Isaiah.

> *"The word 'renew' is actually the word meaning 'exchange.' Exchange means we give up something in order to get something else. So, the idea in the Hebrew is this: we give God our strength, and in exchange, He gives us His! The word 'wait' is the word that carries the idea of intertwining, much like what happens*

> *when we braid hair – the strands are woven together (intertwined) until they are no longer two or three separate strands, but one.*
>
> *"The idea is during the waiting season, God is using that time, and that process, to intertwine our will with His, so when He is finished, and the waiting is done, there are no longer TWO wills, but ONE — His. Waiting is not a passive activity, but an active one. The process is so complete it carries the idea of 'intersection.' It's the place where two roads meet, and in that intersection, it's impossible to tell which road is which. It works that same way in our heart – the intertwining process is so complete, that it's impossible to tell His will from ours – they have become so perfectly One." ~ Teena Goble*

I love that! In the wait, our loving Master bids us to come and abide with Him to find the joy of His presence. Intertwined in the wait, we are intertwined with our God.

Happy sigh....

Many times, I've pictured waiting as a small, confining, difficult place to stand. Yet in the confinement of a wait, God enlarges the step. The steps may seem small through human eyes, but they are never wasted, and are full and free for training, revelation, intimacy, and joy with the Lord.

> *"Blessed are the single-hearted, for they shall enjoy much peace. If you refuse to be hurried and pressed, if you stay your soul on God, nothing can keep you from that clearness of spirit which is life and peace." ~ Amy Carmichael*[106]

- **Write Psalm 27:14**[107].

- **Now write Isaiah 64:4**[108]

Wait for God, take courage as you wait for God, because during the waiting time, God is working. Beyond the waiting time, God will make something amazing happen.

During the forty-year wandering of the Israelites, God gave them a cloud by day and fire by night to guide them.

- **Read Numbers 9:20-22**[109]. **What happened during that time?**

On one hand, I love the guidance of God. On the other hand, I really think I would have had a tough time. Whew, no nesting. No planning. No knowing where we would go and how long we would stay. I've moved thirty-six times and not all of those moves were fun. Packing isn't fun. Unpacking isn't fun. However, each move we kept lightening the load and getting rid of some of the stuff in our lives so we wouldn't need so much stuff.

- **According to Deuteronomy 8:2**[110], **what was the reason?**

Waiting is often a test. Will we be faithful when answers don't come and the way is shrouded in mystery? Will we be faithful to stop when God says stop?

- **Read James 1:2-4**[111] **What happens during testing?**

God's ways are not our ways.[112] His plans and purposes often require waiting, testing, and preparing to produce eternal and completely beautiful results. Waiting is often a getting rid of the things not needed on the next part of a journey, a soul-stilling to have the soul tuned in to God, to prepare the soul for what God has planned.

Abraham waited twenty-five years to receive his promised son. Moses waited forty years in the desert before leading the Israelites out of Egypt.

Joseph had dreams and visions of greatness, but his path led through slavery and dungeons not because of his sin, but because of God's perfect plan.

David was anointed king when he was a young man but had to wait approximately fifteen years before he really became king. Jesus waited approximately thirty years before beginning His earthly ministry.

Waiting is not easy, is often messy and with our earth-bound vision seems without rhyme or reason. However, I'm learning there is an art to waiting and waiting produces art. Sometimes the wait is a beautiful thing like a Rembrandt painting and other times may seem more like a Picasso. The choice of the outcome depends on us.

If I worry, whine, and complain about the wait, the waiting is difficult and messy. If I rest, trust, and praise God during the wait, the waiting is nice and easy. Resting, trusting, and praising God is an art mastered by remembering God's truth.

- **What are we told in Ecclesiastes 3:1?**[113]

- **According to Jeremiah 29:11[114], what kind of plan does God have for you?**

- **Read Jeremiah 17:7-8[115], what happens when you trust God?**

God's timing is perfect, His way is perfect, and trusting Him leads to more trust which always leads to God's perfect results.

If I want something, I would prefer that something as soon as possible. However, if I am crossing a river full of crocodiles, I would be very happy to delay until any large-tooth critters are gone or occupied with something else.

> *"Sometimes living by faith means waiting, giving Him (God) the opportunity to act. A farmer described it to me like this: God tells you to go out on a limb. Once you get out there, you hear a sound—Rrrh! Rrrh! Rrrh! You turn around, and there's the devil with a chain saw, cutting off your limb. Bible faith is staying on the end of that limb and watching Satan continue to saw until the whole tree falls over with him in it and you stay aloft on the limb! That's faith. It's not faith in the tree, nor faith in the limb. It's faith in the Word of God and faith in the One who stands behind His word." ~ Loren Cunningham[116]*

I love a story in 2 Samuel 5 when the Philistines had come to make war with the Israelites and what God told David.

- **Read 2 Samuel 5:23-24[117]. What did God tell David?**

The army got into position and then waited to hear the sound of marching in the top of the balsam trees. I love that story. I love that God's army went before them, and they even heard the sound of God's army.

Y'all when God has us wait, sometimes it's to wait for His protection.

> "God is saying to every Christian, 'You have put your trust in me. Now wait for me!' And when you and I come to a stop and decide that instead of struggling we're going to wait on God, that's when he will begin to work mightily on our behalf!"
> ~ Jim Cymbala

- **Write Psalm 27:14.**[118]

Wait and be confident. Let your heart take courage. Expect God to move in you and through your time of waiting.

> "The greatest things in our spiritual life come out of our waiting hours, when all activity is suspended and the soul learns to be 'silent unto God' while He shapes and molds us for future activities and fruitful years." ~ L. B. Cowman[119]

The coolest thing God has shown me about waiting is, if you live in the moment, you never have to wait.

"I wait for the Lord, my whole being waits, and in his word, I put my hope" (Psalm 130:5 NIV).

> *"To wait upon God is not to sit with folded hands and do nothing, but to wait as men who wait for the harvest. The farmer does not wait idly but with intense activity; he keeps industriously 'at it' until the harvest. To wait upon God is the perfection of activity. We are told to 'rest in the Lord,' not to rust." ~ Oswald Chambers[120]*

Waiting is the "perfection of activity." The ultimate goal is to be conformed to the image of Christ (Romans 8:29) and often waiting is a pressure, the unseen-motion of being molded.

Where we spend our time, who we spend time with, molds us. In the silence of the moments of waiting, there is a call to be still and know that God is God.

Many times, when I visited with a friend, she would scurry and hurry about her house while I was there. I knew she was glad to see me, but she had trouble sitting still. And I'll be honest, it made me sad. I just wanted her to sit and talk with me.

God longs for you to spend time with Him.

Waiting is often a call to our hearts to come and talk with Him, to sit at His feet, to love and be loved. In the rush of life, in the lack of waiting, we miss the moments of precious intimacy.

> *"We cannot go through life strong and fresh on constant express trains with ten minutes for lunch: we must have quiet hours, secret places of the Most High, times of waiting upon the Lord, when we renew our strength and learn to mount up on wings as eagles, and then come back to run and not be weary, and to walk and not faint. The best thing about this stillness is that it gives God a chance to work. 'Anyone who enters God's rest also rests from their works, just as God did from his' (Hebrews 4:10); and when we cease from our thoughts, God's thoughts come*

> *into us; when we get still from our restless activity, 'God...works in [us] to will and to act in order to fulfill his good purpose' (Philippians 2:13), and we have but to work it out. Beloved! Let us take His stillness!"* ~ A. B. Simpson

Breathe deep of the Breath of Life. Still your soul with the One who made your soul. Even when the pathway seems dark, in the long tunnel of waiting, even in the blackness of life's difficulties, let the light of the world light your step and your steps will be light.

> *"There is no music during a musical rest, but the rest is part of the making of the music.... God does not write the music of our lives without a plan. Our part is to learn the tune and not be discouraged during the rests."* ~ L. B. Cowman[121]

"Return to your rest, O my soul, for the Lord has dealt bountifully with you" (Psalm 116:7 NKJV).

Session Four

Storm stability

A young boy ran down the dusty lane to warn his friends that the Bushwhackers were coming. The war had left many women alone, destitute, and fearful.

Praying for protection, Mrs. Walden gathered her family's meager possessions and guns, and placed them under the feather bed. Taking her daughter by the hand, Mrs. Walden dusted the little girl's face with flour, circled her eyes with soot, and laid the tiny, frail girl in bed.

Tears in Mrs. Walden's eyes, she whispered in her precious daughter's ears. "Whatever happens, don't move."

Mrs. Walden hurried to the front porch, sat in the rocking chair, placed a shawl on her lap, and opened the family Bible.

Four men rode into her yard while one man circled around to the back.

Before the bandits could dismount, Mrs. Walden stood. Holding the Bible to her chest, she ran to the one who seemed to be the leader. "Thank you, doctor, for coming. Oh, thank you for coming all of this way."

Drawing their guns, the men with wary eyes scanned the house and yard. They dismounted and cautiously approached the porch.

Mrs. Walden grabbed the leader's arm and pulled him onward. "Hurry sir; it could be the dreaded fever that has taken so many of our neighbors."

The men froze in their tracks and glanced through the screen door. She urged them forward, pushed them through door, and then ordered them to wait while she soaked rags in coal oil for protection against the bad air. The leader took a step back, bumping into those behind.

She continued to beg for help and prodded them onward until they stood in the bedroom. Breathless they stared at the young girl, her face white as snow, black circles around closed eyes.

The girl's eyes flew wide open and a scream of quivering terror filled the room.

The lead man yanked his arm from Mrs. Walden's grasp. Cursing, stumbling, with feet flying they jammed through the doorway, leapt over the front steps, mounted their horses, and disappeared in a cloud of dust.

The story is true. The story is one of God's protection for His children. The story is special because Mrs. Walden was my great-great Grandmother.

Bushwhacking problems storm into our lives seeking to steal and destroy.

Fortunately, Jesus said "I have told you these things, so that **in Me you may have [perfect] peace and confidence**. In the world you have tribulation and trials and distress and frustration; but be of good cheer [**take courage; be confident, certain, undaunted**]! **For I have overcome the world. [I have deprived it of power to harm you and have conquered it for you.**]" (John 16:33 AMPC).

Problems will come, storms will blow into your life, but Jesus is bigger than any storm, and has power over every storm. He will help you through and help you overcome.

> *"You have been chosen. God looks at you and says, 'This one is mine.' Every storm you go through sharpens you. Each mountain you climb strengthens you. God is refining you, perfecting you; calling you into a deeper, more intimate relationship with Him." ~ Rebecca Carrell[122]*

- **Read Matthew 14:25-33[123]. What did Jesus do? What did Peter do?**

Jesus calmed the storm, but before He did, Peter walked on water. Unfortunately, when Peter took his eyes of Jesus, he started to sink. I don't fault Peter, when the storms of life hit, it's so easy to only pay attention to the storms.

The key to storm survival is clinging to the One who calms every storm. When storms hit, cling to Jesus.

When storms hit, don't watch the waves; watch the calmer of the seas (Mark 4:39). Jesus says... "Take courage, it is I; do not be afraid" (Matthew 14:27). Keep your focus on Jesus and walk on the stormy sea (Matthew 14:29). Walk by faith not by sight (2 Corinthians 5:7). Invite Jesus into your boat, and the wind will stop (Matthew 14:32).

When the storms come, God will keep in perfect peace all who trust in Him, all whose thoughts are fixed on Him (Isaiah 26:3).

- **Read Psalm 107:29[124]. What does God do to storms?**

- **According to Isaiah 25:4[125], who is God?**

When the storms come, remember to "fix your thoughts on what is true, and honorable, and right, and pure, and lovely, and admirable. Think about things that are excellent and worthy of praise ... and the God of peace will be with you" (Philippians 4:8-9 NLT).

When the storms come, don't be a wave watcher, wave walk with Jesus.

> *"Jesus Christ is not my security against the storms of life, but He is my perfect security in the storms. He has never promised me an easy passage, only a safe landing." ~ Annie Johnson Flint*

Perspective. I needed perspective on my problems. They are BIG problems, health issues, family members who have gone away from God, financial issues for loved ones, and SO many things were dragging me down and making my heart race.

> *"Live near to God and all things will appear little to you in comparison with eternal realities." ~ Robert Murray M'Cheyne*

To change my view, I downloaded NASA space images on my computer. I now sit and look at galaxies and universes and photos of the earth from space.

Zooming out from my problems, I realize I'm only a miniscule spot in the cosmos and my problems are so very small when I remember how VERY BIG God is!

That's the key. Zoom out! Zoom out from your problems.

> *"Our trials are great opportunities, but all too often we simply see them as large obstacles. If only we would recognize every difficult situation as something God has chosen to prove His love to us, each obstacle would then become a place of shelter and rest, and a demonstration to others of his inexpressible power. If we would look for the signs of His glorious handiwork, then every cloud would indeed become a rainbow, and every difficult mountain path would become one of ascension, transformation, and glorification. If we would look at our past, most of us would realize that the times we endured the greatest stress and felt that every path was blocked were the very times our heavenly Father chose to do the kindest things for us and bestow His richest blessings. God's most beautiful jewels are often delivered in rough packages by very difficult people, but within the package we will find the very treasures of the King's palace and the Bridegroom's love."* ~ A. B. Simpson[126]

In the storms when all is dark, remember God's promises... "I will give you the treasures of darkness and hidden wealth of secret places, so that you may know that it is I, The Lord, the God of Israel, who calls you by your name" (Isaiah 45:3 NASB).

> *"Dear friend, God may send some valuable gifts wrapped in unattractive paper. But do not worry about the wrapping, for you can be sure that inside He has hidden treasures of love,*

> *kindness, and wisdom. If we will simply take what He sends and trust Him for the blessings inside, we will learn the meaning of the secrets of His providence, even in times of darkness." ~ A. B. Simpson*

Pray with me?

God, I'm in a storm and need Your help. Father, thank You that those who dwell in the shelter of the Most High will rest in the shadow of the Almighty. I say, You are my refuge and fortress, the One I can trust (Psalm 91:1-4). Thank You that You are my ever-present help in trouble (Psalm 46:1).

Jesus, as You did for the disciples will you also calm me and calm the storm? Help me to rest in Your love and Your power. May I say with the Psalmist "We went through fire and through water; but You brought us out to rich fulfillment" (Psalm 66:12b NKJV).

> *"No storm where the Master is present will ever overcome you." ~ Henry and Richard Blackaby[127]*

> *"Never fear the rough waters ahead, which through their proud contempt impede your progress. God is greater than the roar of raging water and the mighty waves of the sea. 'The Lord sits enthroned over the flood, the Lord is enthroned as King forever' Psalm 29:10. A storm is simply the hem of His robe, the sign of His coming, and the evidence of His presence. Dare to trust Him! Dare to follow Him! Then discover that the forces that blocked your progress and threatened your life become at His command the very materials He uses to build your street of freedom." ~ F. B. Meyer[128]*

> *"My unmoving mansion of rest is my blessed Lord. Let prospects be blighted; let hopes be blasted; let joy be withered; let mildews destroy everything; I have lost nothing of what I have in God. He is 'my strong habitation whereunto I can continually resort.' I am a pilgrim in the world, but at home in my God. In the earth I wander, but in God I dwell in a quiet habitation." ~ Charles Spurgeon*

Ah friend, no matter how busy your day, how troubled the world, how wild the storm, you have an unmoving mansion of rest in God.

God's calming, comforting hope

I hung up the phone and sighed. Health issues had continued for years and the latest call from the doctor's office continued the search for answers and help. My left breast had been bleeding, and the biopsy results were not yet back in their office.

"Mom!" Our young son burst through the door and beckoned me to hurry. He and his friends had found an injured dove in our neighborhood's small community pool area. We jumped in the car and drove to where the other boys huddled over the small bird.

The left wing of the dove had a small spot of blood and looked a bit crooked. Concern and tenderness etched the boys faces. The dove was not frantic and didn't seem concerned.

I stooped down and gently picked up the soft creature. The dove's tiny heartbeat beat fast, yet the bird didn't try to escape.

The boys, ranging in age from six to thirteen, came closer. In the warm Texas sun, prayers went up for healing and comfort. Sweet prayers. Tender prayers. The little bird's heart quieted.

We searched for shelter for healing and safety.

A fenced-in area under some shrubs was chosen to keep the little bird away from people and dogs. Placing the dove gently on the ground, we quietly backed away and sat in the gazebo near the pool.

Instead of going deeper into the shrubbery, the bird walked toward us, circled around, and sat down without a hint of concern. The boys talked and kept an eye on the small dove. As the sun dipped below the horizon, we locked the gate and left the dove where it would be safe and hopefully heal.

That night as I drifted off to sleep, I thought about the blessing of being able to hold a soft bird. The blessing of being with boys with tender hearts. The blessing of the message from God sending a dove with a hurt left wing as my left breast ached from a biopsy.

As surely as God watches over the birds of the air, I knew God would take care of me. He would carry me to a place of safety and see me through. And, the next day the bird was strong enough to fly away.

Later after a negative diagnosis came, and I needed further surgery, the memory of the dove and God's tender mercies helped me through every new morning.

Whatever you are facing, no matter how broken your wing may be, God's shelter will cover you. His tender mercies are new every morning. Great is God's faithfulness.

- **Have you ever felt like David in Psalm 55:6?** "Oh, that I had wings like a dove! I would fly away and be at rest" (Psalm 55:6).

- **David's lament continues through Psalm 55 as he cries out to God. What does David find as a source of relief when he writes Psalm 55:22?**

    "Cast your burden on the Lord [releasing the weight of it] and He will sustain you; He will never allow the [consistently] righteous to be moved (made to slip, fall, or fail)" (Psalm 55:22 AMPC).

    What happens when we cast our burden on God?

- **What does Peter tell us to do in 1 Peter 5:7[129]? Why?**

The Greek definition of casting is "to throw upon" or "place upon." You don't have to carry the weight of the world or the weight of the many problems you face. Cast your burdens on the Lord and the weight will go off your shoulders and onto God's strong, loving, all-powerful shoulders.

- **Underline the truths about overcoming worry in the following passage.**

    "Don't fret or worry. Instead of worrying, pray. Let petitions and praises shape your worries into prayers, letting God know your concerns. Before you know it, a sense of God's wholeness, everything coming together for good, will come and settle you down. It's wonderful what happens when Christ displaces worry at the center of your life" (Philippians 4:6-7 MSG).

God's comfort is available, but sometimes it's hard to accept when life seems hopeless, when we are weary from the battles of life's difficulties. When hope is placed in earthly dreams, earthly goals, earthly people, and earthly situations, it's easy to get hopeless, and in the dark tunnel of despair, no light can be seen. However, hope eternal comes from anchoring our souls in The Eternal One.

- **What are we told in the following verses?**

- **Psalm 139:12**[130].

- **Psalm 18:28**[131]

- **Psalm 112:4**[132]

- **What promises does Jesus give in the following verses?**

- **John 8:12**[133]

- **John 12:46**[134]

Jesus is our hope, our steadfast and sure assurance that our lives go beyond the temporal to the eternal.

"This hope [this confident assurance] we have as an anchor of the soul [it cannot slip and it cannot break down under whatever pressure bears upon it]—a safe and steadfast hope that enters within the veil [of the heavenly temple, that most Holy Place in which the very presence of God dwells]" (Hebrews 6:19 AMP).

> *"The Christian is strong or weak depending upon how closely he has cultivated the knowledge of God." ~ A.W. Tozer*

Knowing Jesus, knowing God, knowing the character of God, anchors us through the difficulties of life.

Remembering God's power, gives us confidence that God's power will be with us through each day. Remembering who God is, gives us hope for the future.

> *"The primary truth you need to know about God in order for your faith to remain strong is that His love and acceptance is unconditional. When your walk of faith is strong, God loves you. When your walk of faith is weak, God loves you. When you're strong one moment and weak the next, strong one day and weak the next, God loves you. God's love for you is the great eternal constant in the midst of all the inconsistencies of your daily walk." ~ Neil T. Anderson*

I've had reoccurring neck issues, and at times couldn't even glance over one shoulder without great difficulty. Driving was a challenge, but for the safety and well-being of everyone (including myself) I'd force my neck to turn to make sure I could properly see my surroundings.

Checking to verify roads or lanes are clear and looking back is very important, and if not done properly, disaster could happen.

God tells us to look back, to remember His faithfulness, to

remember all the wonderful things He has done for us and for others.

Unfortunately, many people tend to look back at everything negative, at every disaster, heartache, and hard thing they have gone through.

I'm not being flippant about the trials and suffering of life, God knows there are major difficulties. However, we need to remember to look back the right way, to see and remember and praise God for what He has done.

We are to set up markers and memorials higher than the heartaches and failures; higher than all, high enough for our gaze to see God's eternal hope.

Look back and remember God is a faithful God. Remember His rescues, remember the times He helped you through.

Remember God's mercy and grace, remember His goodness, remember His unfailing love, and remember He will never leave you or forsake you.

- **Read and underline the following verses on what we should remember.**

    "He has made His wonders to be remembered; the Lord is gracious and compassionate" (Psalm 111:4 NASB).

    "Remember His wonderful deeds which He has done, His marvels and the judgments from His mouth" (1 Chronicles 16:12 NASB).

    "I shall remember the deeds of the Lord; surely I will remember Your wonders of old" (Psalm 77:11 NASB).

Each time you remember the wonders of God, each time you remember how He has worked in the lives of others, in your own life, your strength will grow, your hope will rise, and your faith will stand stronger.

- **According to Lamentations 3:21-24[135], where is hope found?**

"We put our hope in the Lord. He is our help and our shield" (Psalm 33:20 NLT).

- **Read the passage below, what is the unbreakable spiritual lifeline?**

  "We who have run for our very lives to God have every reason to grab the promised hope with both hands and never let go. It's an unbreakable spiritual lifeline, reaching past all appearances right to the very presence of God where Jesus, running on ahead of us, has taken up his permanent post as high priest for us" (Hebrews 6:18-20 MSG).

The hope in Jesus Christ is eternal, beautiful, and amazing. In the midst of trials, in the midst of heartbreak, in the questions of life, assurance is found in hope eternal. The troubles of today will soon vanish in tomorrow.

Of course, tomorrow can be viewed as a friend or a foe. If we're excited about what is coming, we can't wait for tomorrow. Yay, for tomorrow. Tomorrow is such a wonderful day!

However, if something negative is in the near future, or we think something is going to be negative, poor tomorrow is not talked about in positive terms.

Jesus said to not worry about tomorrow or be anxious for tomorrow, for tomorrow will care for itself (Matthew 6:34). James reminds us we don't have a clue about what will happen tomorrow (James 4:14). God knows the number of our days, He knows the future.

Worrying about tomorrow only causes us to lose today.

When I wake tomorrow, tomorrow will be today, so does tomorrow really exist?

Why should I worry about something that doesn't exist? No wonder tomorrow will care for itself, it kind of vanishes in the light of today.

Tomorrow is just a date that doesn't have a date.

- **Read Psalm 62:8[136]. How many times should we trust God?**

God is good, mighty, and wonderful. You don't have to worry about tomorrow because God is timeless. You can trust Him with all your time. Give your tomorrow to God. Don't put a timeframe on God. No need to worry, have hope for God is here today, He is already in tomorrow, and when you wake in the morning, He will be with you in that day.

During a time of prayer, I saw myself walking and my hands were partially see-through, only a vague outline, visible yet invisible. Since that visual, I sense I'm to move forward releasing any (and all) expectations, not holding anything but God.

"For thus the Lord God, the Holy One of Israel, has said, 'In repentance and **rest** you will be saved, **in quietness and trust is your strength**'" (Isaiah 30:15 NASB).

Walking forward with hands open and down, releasing everything into the care of God; carrying no offenses, no expectations, no anger, no worry, or concerns, we are given freedom. Whatever is done, whatever is now, whatever will come, needs not be carried, but released to God.

Rest in God's comfort. Rest in God's eternal hope. Trust God, know He has the future in His loving hands, and walk unencumbered and free.

> *"I have held many things in my hands, and I have lost them all; but whatever I have placed in God's hands, that I still possess."*
> *~ Corrie Ten Boom*

- **Can you think of a time when in the midst of a trial you became aware of God's loving presence? In what ways did He make His presence known? Was it through an answered prayer, the beauty of a sunset or perhaps through some loving words from a friend? When you look back on your life do you see God's faithfulness and grace?**

    Whatever your answer, please make the time to remember all the ways God has worked in your life. Reflecting on God's grace will give you faith and hope for the future.

> *"Your possessions are never so safe as when you are willing to resign them, and you are never so rich as when you put all you have into the hand of God."* ~ *Charles Spurgeon*

"May our Lord Jesus Christ himself and God our Father, who loved us and by his grace gave us eternal encouragement and good hope, encourage your hearts, and strengthen you in every good deed and word. He saved us, not because of righteous things we had done, but because of his mercy. He saved us through the washing of rebirth and renewal by the Holy Spirit, whom he poured out on us generously through Jesus Christ our Savior, so that, having been justified by his grace, we might become heirs having the hope of eternal life" (2 Thessalonians 2:16-17, Titus 3:5-7 NIV).

"For the mountains may be removed and the hills may shake, but My lovingkindness will not be removed from you, and My covenant of peace will not be shaken, says the Lord who has compassion on you" (Isaiah 54:10 NASB).

Resting need

"God has told his people, 'Here is a place of rest; let the weary rest here. This is a place of quiet rest.' But they would not listen" (Isaiah 28:12 NLT).

At times I've thought something was missing in my life, something I wanted or needed. I'd stare and whine at the missing piece which only caused me to miss God's peace. When the focus was only on what I thought was missing, my soul was so restless that I missed seeing God's provision.

How often are we focused on what we think we need, or perhaps what we really do need, while all the time, all around us, God is already providing?

Eve knew this problem. She had been given the perfect place to live, the perfect husband, perfect intimacy with her husband and with God, and yet she lost it all because one thing captured her attention. One thing looked delightful, she thought she needed one more thing, was missing something, and that one thing caused her to lose all things.

We all have our needs. We are a needy people.

It's very easy to think a *want* is a *need*. When something is wanted and becomes consuming, desperation can lead to bad choices, bad friendships, and bad relationships. Even Godly desires can quickly turn dark, heavy, and consuming.

I know, because of moving thirty-six times, because of the difficulties in my past, because of my own desires, I've at times been desperate for friendships, for a safe place, for a settled home, for a relationship that would fill my neediness. Unfortunately, because of that desperation, bad choices were made. At times I even sought Godly friendships but became so consumed with the friendships that I lost sight of God.

Anything or anyone, that turns the focus off of God, that becomes bigger than the desire for God, can lead to unrest and/or ungodly decisions. God is the safe place. God is the friend needed. God has all we need. God is the resting place. God is the answer to every need.

While Jesus walked the earth, people in great need came to Him. Jesus healed, raised people from the dead, provided food in amazing ways, walked on water, and then rose Himself from the dead. Our Savior can do anything for nothing is impossible for God.

As an example of something needed, a large crowd had come to Jesus for healing.

The hour was late, and the disciples suggested that Jesus send the crowd away to go to neighboring villages to get something to eat.

Jesus responded, "They do not need to go away; you give them something to eat. And they said to Him, '**We have** here **only** five loaves and two fish.' He said, '**Bring them** here **to Me**'" (Matthew 14:16-18).

Jesus took that tiny offering and filled the needs of over 5000 men along with women and children, and still had twelve basket full left over. The need was real, the need was huge, but with God all things are possible. When a need is brought to Jesus, Jesus fills that need in amazing ways.

What happens when a need is brought to Jesus?

- **Read Mark 4:37-39[137]. What happened?**

- **Read Matthew 9:18-25[138]. What need was brought to Jesus, how did He meet that need?**

- **Read Luke 23:33-43[139]. What need was asked of Jesus, what was His reply?**

- **Read Matthew 15:30-31[140]. What needs were brought to Jesus and how did He meet their needs?**

Jesus calms the storms, raises the dead to life, gives the sinner eternal life, heals the sick, the lame walk, the blind see, the mute talk, and God receives glory.

Every need brought to Jesus was met by Jesus.

- **Read the excerpt from Mark 10:46-52 below. What did the man need? How did Jesus meet his need?**

"...blind Bartimaeus, sat by the road begging. And when he heard that it was Jesus of Nazareth, he began to cry out and say, 'Jesus, Son of David, have mercy on me!' Then many warned him to be quiet; but he cried out all the more, 'Son of David, have mercy on me!' So, Jesus stood still and commanded him to be called.... Bartimaeus, throwing aside his garment, rose and came to Jesus. So, Jesus answered and said to him, 'What do you want Me to do for you?' The blind man said to Him, 'Rabboni, that I may receive my sight.' Then Jesus said to him, 'Go your way; your faith has made you well.' And immediately he received his sight and followed Jesus on the road" (Mark 10:46-52 NKJV).

Bartimaeus kept crying out for mercy, he didn't let others dissuade him, and then he threw off his garment, came to Jesus and asked for his sight to be restored. Then, when healed, he followed Jesus.

Did you catch that Jesus asked Bartimaeus what he wanted? Jesus knew, but in asking, He gave Bartimaeus an opportunity to voice his need and then to see his specific request answered.

Whatever your need, keep asking Jesus, throw off anything that hinders you, ask specifically, and follow Him.

Our pastor when we lived in Idaho shared when someone came to him for prayer, he would ask specific questions to find out how they would like for him to pray. God knows our every need and is never limited by our lack of communication skills or method of praying. I've had times all I could do was pray, "Help!" Thankfully, the Holy Spirit is there to intercede and translate every request (see Romans 8:26-27[141]).

Sometimes when I stumble through a prayer not sure really how to ask or what to ask, I take great comfort knowing the Holy Spirit is probably leaning over to God and saying, "This is what she means..."

I wonder if the times I throw up a prayer, or don't come to God with more than a vague request, will I see how God is working and answering? If a request is specific, I know when God has specifically answered. If I pray, "Please bless my friend" God's blessings may come (and will come) in various ways, but will I even notice the answers?

If my request takes on a more direct manner, "Please bless _____ with the blessing of opening their heart to know You as Lord and Savior," I now have a tangible way to watch how God moves.

By drilling down to understand what we are asking, we know better the true need, and then later can see the ways God answers.

When you are able, ask specifically, record your request, and you too will be able to see the amazing ways God leads, provides, comforts, and works in your life and the lives of others.

Bring your need to Jesus. No matter how big or small, bring your need to Jesus. With Jesus, needs are met, thousands are fed, storms are stilled, the dead are raised to life, the sinner is given forgiveness, the lame walk, the blind see, and the illness leaves.

Seek Jesus for your need.

Offer your prayers, offer yourself, offer what you have to Jesus, and watch Him work in wonderful ways.

- **Read the passage below and underline and note what happens when we seek God.** "...our heavenly Father knows that you need all these things. But seek first His kingdom and His righteousness, and all these things will be added to you" (Matthew 6:32b - 33 NASB).

- **In the verses below, underline the truth of God's gracious giving.**

   "For the Lord God is a sun and shield; the Lord will give grace and glory; no good thing will He withhold from those who walk uprightly" (Psalm 84:11 NKJV).

   "The young lions lack and suffer hunger; but those who seek the Lord shall not lack any good thing" (Psalm 34:10 NKJV).

- **Read Philippians 4:19[142], how many needs will be met?**

- **According to Romans 8:32[143], how many things will God give?**

- **Underline how many things will God perform.** "I will cry out to God Most High, to God who performs all things for me" (Psalm 57:2 NKJV).

- **According to James 1:17[144], how many good things and how many perfect gifts are given by God?**

"The Lord will always lead you. **He will satisfy your needs** in dry lands and give strength to your bones. You will be like a garden that has much water, like a spring that never runs dry" (Isaiah 58:11 NCV).

The truth is, God will meet all our needs. He doesn't withhold any good thing, and every good thing comes from His loving hand.

> *"When Christ lives in you, He brings every divine resource with Him. Every time you face a need, you meet it with the presence of the crucified, risen, and triumphant Lord of the universe inhabiting you." ~ Henry and Richard Blackaby[145]*

When we seek God and His will, when we hunger and thirst for righteousness, we will be filled. God fills the empty places when we pursue Him.

Is there something in your life that has captured your attention? What do you hope for, long for, and don't think you can live without? What do you need? Be specific. If something is vague, drill down to the root. Find what is behind the need. A need can quickly become an idol. Whatever draws our attention to the point we are without rest.

The other morning, I had a long list of needs I laid out in prayer to God. I'm learning when I truly believe God will meet ALL my needs, my prayers take on a different tone. My soul can rest in the wait, in the longing for things to change, to be fixed, people to be healed, or provision to come...

What do you need?
Money?
Friendships?
A spouse?
A child?
A job?
A better job, a bigger paycheck, a new place to live?
A person, a thing, a place, a healthy dose of chocolate....
Pray with me?

Heavenly Father, I need ...

_____
_____
_____

God, I know nothing I need is bigger than what You can provide. I don't know how this need will be met, but I trust that You can meet all my needs.

Will You show me, Father? Will You show me how You are working? Will You reveal Your truth to combat the unrest in my soul in regard to this need? Please help me refocus my focus on Your kingdom perspective.

Help me to remember in my weakness, Your grace is sufficient (2 Corinthians 12:9).

In my troubles, help me remember Jesus You have overcome the world (John 16:33).

Help me to remember in my trials, that You will stand with me and never leave or forsake me (Psalm 94:14).

Help me to remember in the fire, in the floods, You will be with me and will not allow me to be overwhelmed (Isaiah 43:2).

God, help me to remember in my need for provision, You own the cattle on the thousand hills, and You provide in amazing ways (Psalm 50:10).

Help me to remember when the burden for my needs are so very heavy, Jesus Your yoke is soul light and never oppressive (Matthew 11:30).

When I need a friend, help me to remember Jesus has called me friend (John 15:15).

When I am alone, (even in a marriage), single, divorced, or widowed, help me to remember God is an unfailing husband (Isaiah 54:5), an unfailing Father to the fatherless, and an unfailing defender of widows and orphans (Psalm 68:5, Deuteronomy 10:18).

When I need someone to talk to and need advice, help me to remember You are always available (Jeremiah 33:3).

When I need someone to rescue me, help me to remember Your arm is never too short to save (Isaiah 59:1).

For all my needs, help me to rest my needs at Your feet, Jesus. Help me to remember every answer is found in Your love and every need I have will be met by Your loving hand.

Thank You, Father. I ask these things in the mighty name of Your Son, Jesus Christ.

Amen.

Circumstantial rest

Many times, I've felt caged by circumstances. Caged by illness or caged waiting for change to come or caged by thoughts and worries. I've been like a racehorse trapped at the starting gate.

During those times, I have, cried, kicked, and bashed against the confining boundaries. If only, I could run free, I would be happy and satisfied.

My visual is not a pretty picture. Being antsy and frustrated at not being able to do what I want to do or go where I want to go have left my little racehorse-self battered and bruised. Jesus says come to Him and He gives rest.

I picture the Lord sitting in the stands at the racetrack and watching. I'm having a fit at not being able to run, but then I realize God placed the boundaries around me.

God's boundaries are always tender with His love.

Now, when I envision my little racehorse self at the starting gate, I notice the enclosure is padded securely with God's love.

- **Read the following verses and underline the truths of God's boundaries.**

"You have enclosed me behind and before and laid Your hand upon me. Such knowledge is too wonderful for me; it is too high, I cannot attain to it" (Psalm 139:5-6 NASB).

"Lord, you alone are my portion and my cup; you make my lot secure. The boundary lines have fallen for me in pleasant places; surely I have a delightful inheritance" (Psalm 16:5-6 NIV).

When God's boundaries are around you, in the confining of your circumstantial rest, you are tenderly held tight in the unfailing love of God. Choose to rest and choose to trust God even when you can't see how He is working and what is happening.

- **Read 2 Kings 6:8-17[146]. When the servant first looked at the situation, what did he see surrounding them? What did he see when his eyes were opened?**

- **What does Paul tell us in 2 Corinthians 4:18[147]?**

Beyond our earthly vision, God is moving in the eternal for eternal purposes.

When I was younger and horrible things happened and no one was there to help, my Father God held me close and loved me back to life.

During times of illness and surgeries, when I couldn't do anything, couldn't move physically, God helped my spirit soar in the freedom of His presence.

When I felt confined in a new location without friends and family, I discovered more of the friendship and relationship with God.

God's boundaries have kept me from making bad mistakes and from pursuing things I thought I wanted. His boundaries have kept me from things I thought I was ready to handle. Looking back, I realize God saved me from embarrassing disaster.

Sometimes we feel confined and held captive by things that don't exist. We can easily confine ourselves behind an electric, invisible fence of our own making, or confined by what someone else has told us.

When I was a little girl and we went on road trips. I would look at the map, then watch the road and wait in anticipation to see the boundary lines on the states. I was disappointed when there never were any. The lines didn't exist on the ground, they were man-made on the map.

At times, I confined myself by thinking I needed to act a certain way, talk, walk, do everything a certain way to be a "good" Christian. I felt guilty if I didn't have a quiet time, then felt guilty if my quiet time wasn't long enough, or if I would spend too much time doing one thing and not another thing. Guilt confined me in until I couldn't move or breathe and I lost my joy. Gasp, wheeze...

- **Read Luke 10:38-42[148]. What did Mary do and what did Jesus say about her choice?**

Martha had confined herself to what she could "do" for Jesus instead of choosing to rest at the feet of Jesus. Mary chose the better way.

We don't have to be confined by service or by our ideas (or someone else's ideas) of how we should look or what we should do for Christ.

Rest at the feet of Jesus. Whatever your circumstance, whatever your situation, you can come to the feet of Jesus.

There is a beautiful, unconfining simplicity of life with God.

- **Read Micah 6:8[149]. What has God told us to do?**

Do what is right, love mercy and walk humbly with God. I wonder if God just wants me to open my eyes and tell Him good morning and that I love Him.

Let's crawl out of earthly man-made confinements, walk with God, and enjoy Him.

> **Read the following verse.** "Now the Lord is the Spirit, and where the Spirit of the Lord is present, there is freedom. And we all, with unveiled faces reflecting the glory of the Lord, are being transformed into the same image from one degree of glory to another, which is from the Lord, who is the Spirit." 2 Corinthians 3:17-18 (NET Bible)

- **What is present with the Spirit of the Lord? What are we reflecting?**

Unconfinement comes as we realize we are not created to look like clones of one another, we are to allow Christ to mold us into His image. His image is unique, beautiful, fluid, glorious, and never confined or molded to man's ideals or image.

"Christ has set us free to live a free life. So, take your stand! Never again let anyone put a harness of slavery on you" (Galatians 5:1 MSG). (Or confine you!)

- **In Mark 12:30-31[150], what did Jesus say was the greatest commandment?**

We are God's unique, glorious creations, created to love God and love others.

> *"All we really have to do is to love God and rejoice in Him."*
> *~ Brother Lawrence.*

The other day I pondered about our amazing bodies. Blood travels throughout the body, then returns to the heart and lungs to receive oxygen which regenerates, renews, restores, and refreshes.

In the same way, when we are told to love the Lord with all our hearts, the lifeblood of our heart is regenerated, renewed, restored, and refreshed through the loving heart of the Breath of Life.

In loving the Lord with all your heart, soul, strength, and mind, life makes sense, because true life is found in The One who brings life. Love God and you are freed from the praise of man, freed from trying to please others.

When God is the first love, He fills the empty places, freeing from worry, anxiety, stress over today and tomorrow.

Love the Lord your God with all...

> ***your heart*** ... your heart finds home, comfort, and love.
>
> ***your soul*** ... your soul aligns, centers, and finds rest.
>
> ***your strength*** ... your strength becomes mighty in God's might.
>
> ***your mind*** ... your mind becomes focused, single-minded on God, in the peace of God.

In loving God, in giving all to God, you receive back His love and become fulfilled and filled with His all. In loving God, time slows to its proper speed in the light of eternity. Evil thoughts are taken captive and destroyed in the light of God's truth. When you love God with all, you are freed to live and love above all that is on the earth because you are seated in the heavenlies.

Loving God, abiding in God's love is freedom to be loved in the eternal security of His unfailing love. Love the Lord your God above all, and all you needs are met, all your questions are answered knowing God's love will provide.

Whatever your circumstance, rest in the freedom of God's unfailing love.

> *"Do not let anything set your heart beating so fast as love for Him. Let this ambition fire your soul; may this be the foundation of every enterprise upon which you enter, and your sustaining motive." ~ Charles Spurgeon*

Session Five

Session Five: The Forgotten Resting Place

Resting equipped

In the early 1970's members of the oldest Sunday school class at a large Houston church decided they wanted to help Boy's Country, a Christian home for boys.

These ladies, along with their friends from their Sunday School class of women seventy and over, divided and repotted their plants at home, set up a garage sale and used proceeds to approach a large rancher in the Houston area to buy cows.

The manager took one look at their meager funds, declined their offer to make up the shortfall with monthly payments of $30.00 and sent them down the road.

The women were not deterred. They drove to the next ranch and approached the owner.

Mrs. Hadlow spoke to the man in her slow, precise Mississippi voice, "Now there is a children's home that needs some cattle for the children. We have almost three hundred dollars and we want to buy a registered cow and a heifer calf" with a pause of embarrassment...she continued in an even quieter, and most sincere voice... "and we would like for the cow to be expecting again."

The man had bought and sold many cattle in his life, he knew good cattle and knew how to drive a hard bargain. But, standing before this little group of waiting ladies, he was stymied.

The women just stood there, anticipating his positive response. He didn't have the heart to tell them one of his calves was worth more than what they were offering.

However, within a week the man arranged for a round-up of his choice cattle, had his men pen them for inspection, then stood aside and waited as the ladies stood on the bottom board of a corral looking over the milling cattle.

The man stood aside, patiently waiting. Mrs. Hadlow turned to him. "are these good ones?"

With a small smile tugging at the corners of his mouth "Yes, ma'am, these are my best."

She nodded. "Then, we will take three of them. We have saved and collected some more money. We don't have it all today, but we will pay you out the rest."

The man paled but agreed. Later, he said he had never seen more loving people who wanted to help others.

Because of these women, a good-sized herd was established, providing meat and opportunities for the boys to learn ranch management, meat cutting, and caring for animals.

The women weren't wealthy, they didn't have much to offer, but they trusted in the God who owns cattle on a thousand hills. They trusted in a God who feeds thousands with a few loaves and fishes.

These women trusted in a God who uses little boys to slay giants. They trusted in God who used 300 to defeat a humongous Midianite army.

Will you trust God to be faithful to use what you have been given? Will you believe in the supernatural power, supernatural provision, and supernatural quipping of God?

Throughout the Bible God blesses His children with awe-inspiring, jaw-dropping power and creativity. The story of Bazelel fascinates me. Who was he and why was he hand-picked by God? Chapter after chapter in Exodus tells what Bazelel crafted and created.

"Moses then said to the Israelites: 'Look, the Lord has appointed by name Bezalel son of Uri, son of Hur, of the tribe of Judah. He has filled him with God's Spirit, with wisdom, understanding, and ability in every kind of craft to design artistic works in gold, silver, and bronze, to cut gemstones for mounting, and to carve wood for work in every kind of artistic craft. He has also given both him and Oholiab son of Ahisamach, of the tribe of Dan, the ability to teach others" (Exodus 35:30-34 NASB).

What Bazelel accomplished was amazing because of amazing God.

- **According to Exodus 36:1[151], what did God give these men?**

When God wants a job done, He can do it Himself, but so very often He chooses someone for an assignment. When little David killed the giant Goliath, little David didn't morph into a bigger giant, he relied on the giant strength of God (1 Samuel 17:45-51).

When Gideon defeated the Midianites, it wasn't because of his power, but the power of God (Judges 7:19-22).

Moses didn't part the Red Sea under his own power, but because of God's power (Exodus 14).

Samson killed a thousand men with the jawbone of a donkey (Judges 15:14-15). That jawbone didn't give Samson the power and ability, God equipped him with the power and ability.

- **According to Matthew 17:20, how much faith will move a mountain?**[152]

God gives wisdom, strength, and God gives the ability. Small steps of faith lead to mighty moves of God. Step forward in faith, confident in the knowledge that what God calls you to do, He has equipped you to do in His power.

- **Read Ephesians 3:20**[153]**. How and what does God provide?**

When God equips you through His power, He does exceedingly, superabundantly more than you could ask, imagine, or think. The original Greek definition for equipping is much bigger and even more exciting than I imagined. According to Strong's G2675 – katartizō (Equipping or perfecting) means to render, to mend, to repair, to complete, put in order, arrange, adjust, prepare, ethically: to strengthen, perfect, complete, make one what he ought to be, frame, restore, make perfect.

Isn't that cool? God's equipping is multi-functional, on-going, constantly adjusting, refitting, repairing, mending, setting right, restoring, to make you perfectly fitted for His assignments. Now that's some awesome equipping!

And the more we read God's word, the more we are further equipped.

- **Read 2 Timothy 3:16-17[154]. Why is scripture important? In what way does it equip?**

Knowing God's Word gives the power to know God's power and how His power works within you.

God's gifts come to us all. "He gave some as apostles, and some as prophets, and some as evangelists, and some as pastors and teachers, for the equipping of the saints for the work of service, to the building up of the body of Christ" (Ephesians 4:11-12 NASB).

- **Read Philippians 2:13[155]. Who is at work in you? Why?**

- **According to 2 Corinthians 9:8[156], how much grace will God give? What will your sufficiency be and for how many things?**

You aren't just equipped, you are super-abundantly, powerfully, exceedingly more than you can ask or imagine, awe-inspiring, jaw-dropping equipped with God's divine, miracle-working power, for ALL things through the MIGHTY power of Christ!

- **According to Psalm 73:25-26[157], where is your unending strength found?**

- **What are we told in Ephesians 6:10?[158] Where do we find strength?**

God by the action of His power at work within you, is able to carry out His purpose and do superabundantly, far over and above all that you dare ask or think infinitely beyond your highest prayers, desires, thoughts, hopes, or dreams.

Far too often I've thought I didn't have what I needed, or know the right connections, or have the speaking ability, writing ability, ability in any ability, so I wasn't completing anything because I was so busy thinking I was missing something and in need of something.

"The Lord said to him, 'What is that in your hand?' And he said, 'A staff'" (Exodus 4:2 NASB) Moses held a simple shepherd's staff, only a piece of wood, surely, he didn't have what was needed to go against Pharaoh and the armies of Egypt. However, God used Moses, and that simple piece of wood, in mighty ways to show God's power.

> *"The first habit to form is the habit of realizing the provision God has made." ~ Oswald Chambers*

Just as God asked Moses to look at what was in his hand, I need to open my eyes to see what God has already given.

Hmmm, so what is in my hand? I believe God called me to write and that talent, came from God. However, I need to use what God has given.

Instead of looking at my shortcomings, or anything I think I'm lacking, I need instead to focus on God and allow Him to use me in the ways He chooses.

> *"The most healthy state of a Christian is always to be empty of self and constantly depending upon the Lord for provision; to be consistently poor in self and rich in Jesus; to be weak as water personally, but mighty through God to do great exploits."*
> *~ Charles Spurgeon*

Nothing is impossible for God, He is faithful to complete the work He began in you. God's provision always comes. It's not your might or your power, but by God's Spirit, giving strength, equipping, and empowering. God uses the weak to show His might, and He will give you all you need to complete what you are called to complete.

- **Read the following verses. Where is power in the Christian life found? What kind of power is available to us as Christians?**

    "We have this treasure in clay jars, so that the extraordinary power belongs to God and does not come from us. ... The power that is working within us is able to do far beyond all that we ask or think" (2 Corinthians 4:7, Ephesians 3:20 NET).

God equips you. Another amazing gift God gives, is that He will fill you up so that in your filling you can pour out to others.

- **What does Jesus say in John 15:5?**[159]

Abide with Jesus, and the fruit bears in abundance.

No need to ever feel empty when you are in Christ Jesus. For when you abide with Jesus, you are filled to the brim with His joy.

- **In the following verses, underline the filling.**

    "I will be filled with joy because of You. I will sing praises to Your name, O Most High" (Psalm 9:2 NLT).

    "The LORD is my strength and shield. I trust him with all my heart. He helps me, and my heart is filled with joy. I burst out in songs of thanksgiving" (Psalm 28:7 NLT).

    "But may all who search for You be filled with joy and gladness in you. May those who love your salvation repeatedly shout, 'The LORD is great!'" (Psalm 40:16 NLT).

    "Like your name, O God, your praise reaches to the ends of the earth; Your right hand is filled with righteousness" (Psalm 48:10 NIV).

    "Happy are the people you choose and invite to stay in your court. We are filled with good things in Your house, Your holy Temple" (Psalm 65:4 NCV).

"The whole earth is filled with awe at Your wonders; where morning dawns, where evening fades, You call forth songs of joy" (Psalm 65:8 NIV).

"But let the godly rejoice. Let them be glad in God's presence. Let them be filled with joy" (Psalm 68:3 NLT).

"But may all who search for You be filled with joy and gladness in You. May those who love your salvation repeatedly shout, 'God is great!'" (Psalm 70:4 NLT).

"My mouth is filled with Your praise, declaring your splendor all day long" (Psalm 71:8 NIV).

"Let them give thanks to the Lord for His lovingkindness, and for His wonders to the sons of men! For He has satisfied the thirsty soul, and the hungry soul He has filled with what is good" (Psalm 107:8-9 NASB).

"Blessed are those who hunger and thirst for righteousness, for they shall be filled" (Matthew 5:6 NKJV).

Jesus is the fullness who "fills all in all" (Ephesians 1:23).

The love of Christ surpasses knowledge and fills to "all the fullness of God" (Ephesians 3:19).

Jesus said, "I have told you these things so that you will be filled with My joy. Yes, your joy will overflow!" (John 15:11 NLT)

Let's be like the disciples who were "continually filled with joy and with the Holy Spirit" (Acts 13:52)

- **Based on the scripture you have read and underlined, when you think about the task you have been given, where will you find the power needed, and how much power will be given?**

Whether you work at home raising children, work as a caretaker, work at a job away from home, wherever you work, whatever you are called to do for this season or for the long-term, be assured God will equip you for all that you need.

Remember also, God equips you and God will equip your children and grandchildren for whatever is needed.

Rest in the knowledge that in Christ, you are super-abundantly equipped. You are filled to all fullness with the power of God to joyfully accomplish all God has asked you to accomplish.

Be who God created you to be, do what God called you to do, live, truly live your life in Christ and allow His power to work in you and through you.

Power praise refreshing

Dragging my tail, I felt far from God, desperate for His touch. My sweet husband had searched for a job for eight months. School started for our son in twelve days, and our life remained stagnant in one big waiting and holding pattern.

A gentle voice nudged in my spirit, "**Praise Me**."

I'll be honest, I didn't jump right in. After a few minutes of hesitation, I turned on praise music. As the songs played, I joined in the praise. Slowly at first. Then as I allowed the music to wash over my weary soul, happy goose bumps popped on my arms and God's presence engulfed me.

I wondered are we made to praise? Do we need praise like we need sleep and food? Is that what feeds our soul? Yes! To get through the problems of today, we are equipped with a safety device–Praise. Praise really does work. It's like a soul parachute that catches us as we fall and uplifts our soul.

I've pulled the praise rip cord many times during difficult seasons, and without fail I've received comfort and hope. Sometimes, praise brings a good, cleansing cry.

Other times during praise, gloom and doom is replaced with joy.

Praise provides reassurance as we nestle closer to God, and the best part — praise takes focus off the problems and back on our almighty, healing, gracious, compassionate, restoring God. Don't ever discount the power of praise.

- **What happened in 2 Chronicles 20:22[160] when they began to sing and praise?**

- **Read the following verse and note what happened.** Paul and Silas were beaten and thrown in prison, and yet they praised God singing hymns and praising. While they were praising... "Suddenly, there was a massive earthquake, and the prison was shaken to its foundations. All the doors immediately flew open, and the chains of every prisoner fell off!" And then, the jailer and all his household were saved (Acts 16:25-34 NCV).

The power of praise sets the prisoner free, and not only sets those free who are praying and praising, praise also has a mighty domino effect. There is GREAT power in praise beyond what we can imagine or conceive.

> *"Praise pierces the darkness, dynamites long standing obstructions, and sends the demons of hell fleeing."*
> *~ Wesley L. Duewel*

In the praise of your awesome God, you will find the awesome power of God.

The victory over Jericho came with a shout of praise. "the people shouted when the priests blew the trumpets. And it happened when the people heard the sound of the trumpet, and the people shouted with a great shout, that the wall fell down flat. Then the people went up into the city, every man straight before him, and they took the city (Joshua 6:20 NKJV).

> *"Praise is the Christian's heavy artillery. Praise is more effective in spiritual warfare than is an atom bomb in military battle."*
> *~ Wesley Duewel*[61]

Praise is a powerful gift for the believer. The writer of Hebrews tells us, "let us continually offer the sacrifice of praise to God, that is, the fruit of our lips, giving thanks to His name" (Hebrews 13:15 NKJV).

The devil often tries to convince us that praising God during a difficult time doesn't make sense. The reason Satan doesn't want us praising God during hard times, because praise releases the power of God.

The other day, while I walked and listened to praise music, I was caught up in the joy of worship. I felt like my hair was standing on end. (Really! I even stopped and took a selfie to check.) No outward signs, but what delight as my spirit soared to the heavens. My feet were touching earth but my soul defied gravity.

- **Read Ephesians 2:6. As a Christian, where are you seated?**

Jesus said the truth will set us free. So, if we could truly grasp the truth that our souls live in the heavens, our soul-feet would never touch the ground. We would be walking on air – Holy Spirit air.

Through praise and worship, filling our thoughts with God's Word, meditating on the goodness of God, we defy gravity. We are never earth-bound when we are heaven-bound.

I love what Levi Lusko shared in reference to Paul in prison.

> *"There are two sides to every chain. He didn't look at the situation and go 'I'm chained to this guard.' He looked and said, 'the guard is chained to me. He can't go anywhere.'"*
> *~ Levi Lusko*

I love that! It's easy to stare so long at the chains in our lives that we miss our God-given opportunities.

- **Again, please. Underline how many things God will work to the good.** "And we know that all things work together for good to those who love God, to those who are the called according to His purpose" (Romans 8:28 NKJV).

Throughout the study we've looked at Romans 8:28, because we need to know, and always remember, that ***good will come because of our good God***! Remembering that truth, gives us the ability to praise God during everything.

> *"In Africa a tree produces the 'taste berry,' a unique fruit that literally alters taste buds so that everything that's eaten after eating the berry tastes good and sweet. Praise is the 'taste berry' of the Christian's life. When our hearts are filled with praise, when we choose to praise God, no matter what, stress fades into the background of a battle won before it begins, life is sweet, and all is good."* ~ *Mary Southerland*

When we see our difficult situations in the light of our all-mighty God, we see things from a different perspective.

In the middle of the night I woke worried about an extended family member. Flopping, tossing, and turning I took my concerns to God, or should I say I wrestled with my concerns and hoped God was listening. Then it hit me, I needed to remember to pray and praise.

- **In the verse below, underline what happens when we pray with thanksgiving?**

   "Don't worry about anything; instead, pray about everything. Tell God what you need and thank him for all he has done. Then you will experience God's peace, which exceeds anything we can understand. His peace will guard your hearts and minds as you live in Christ Jesus." Philippians 4:6-7 (NLT)

Praying and thanking God brings the peace of God. As I took my worry to God and turned the request into a praise, the focus changed from worry to praise, the prayers became bigger, and the strength became bigger, and the comfort became bigger, and the peace became bigger, and the knowledge of God's might and power became bigger. The problems that loomed so very large at the beginning became tiny in the presence of Almighty, loving, all-magnificent, creator of the universe, nothing-is-impossible God.

I flipped my concerns into praises. My prayer changed from... "God, _____ is in a bad situation and relationship please help them."

To... "God, thank You that no situation is too big for You. I praise You that nothing is impossible for You. Thank You that You love _____ more than I can fathom. Praise You that You know the number of their days and Your plans are good for them (Psalm 139:16, Jeremiah 29:11).

Praise You, God that I can place _____ into Your loving hands and ask that You work mighty in their situation and draw them close to You. Praise You. O Lord God, You have begun to show Your servant Your greatness and Your strong hand; for what god is there in heaven or on earth who can do such works and mighty acts as Yours? (Deuteronomy 3:24).

God, how I praise You that the relationship _____ wants and needs is found in You. Praise You that You illumine the darkness and are a light for their path (Psalm 18:28, Psalm 119:105). Show them Your way, Father. Praise You that you will direct them in the way of wisdom and lead them on an upright path (Proverbs 4:11).

Praise You and thank You that I can come to You with my request. Thank You, Father for Your unfailing love.

I ask these things in the name of Your Son, Jesus Christ who is my Savior. Amen.

- **What situation are you facing? How can you turn your prayer request into a praise request?**

Resting in the power of prayer

Have you ever heard someone say, "All we can do is pray?" All we can do is pray, should be turned into "Praise God, we can pray!"

We can bring **all** our requests to God. We should be grateful, excited, ecstatic about our ability to come to our all-powerful, all-loving God with requests.

Prayer is such a gift, a blessing to talk with our holy God, our Father God, and bring our requests and intercede for others.

What if you knew your prayers made a difference?

What if you remembered who God is, the power available to you, the power that works in you?

> *"Do we know the power of our supernatural weapon? Do we dare to use it with the authority of a faith that commands as well as asks? God baptize us with holy audacity and divine confidence! He is not wanting great men, but He is wanting men who will dare to prove the greatness of their God. But God! But prayer!"* ~ A. B. Simpson

One night I dreamed I was praying with several people and not one of them paid attention to my prayers. Then I really prayed, heart-felt, passionate prayers, begging God for His help. Immediately lives were changed before my very eyes.

I woke and pondered how often I pray half-hearted prayers. I wondered how often results are not accomplished or unseen, because of the lack of passion and consistency in praying.

> *"Heaven pays little attention to casual requests. God is not moved by feeble desires, listless prayers, and spiritual laziness. God rejoices to see a soul on fire with holy passion as the heart reaches out to Him. White-hot prayer burns its way through obstacles to the throne of God. A burning heart is your best preparation for prayer. Fiery prayer is the intensity born of the Holy Spirit. The fire of the Spirit baptizes your heart as a prayer warrior and empowers your praying. If your prayers are not touched with holy fire, you have not yet felt the heartbeat of God. To be absorbed in God's will, God's purpose, God's zeal, and God's glory will set your heart and prayer aflame. Prayer feeds on flame. It is the fiery intercessors who conquer. Such burning desire makes intercession invincible. Desire is the flame within; intercession is the flame leaping out to God."*
> ~ *Wesley Duewel*[162]

Read that quote again. When praying, pray earnestly, and pray white-hot prayers.

- **Underline what happens when we pray heartfelt, earnest prayers.** "The earnest (heartfelt, continued) prayer of a righteous man makes tremendous power available [dynamic in its working]" (James 5:16b AMP).

The King James Version says, "The effectual fervent prayer of a righteous man availeth much."

- **Read the Greek definition below and underline what comes from effectual, fervent prayer.**

    The Greek definitions for effectual, fervent, and availeth means to put forth power, to be hot, to boil, to glow, to be strong, to have power as shown by extraordinary deeds, to exert, wield power, to have strength to overcome, to be a force.

You are given the opportunity for powerful, white-hot, glowing, strong, extraordinary power and overcoming strength, to be a force in your prayers.

Throughout the Bible and throughout history, prayers have routed enemies, saved lives, and altered the destiny of nations. Holy and exalted, God loves us enough to give us the amazing blessing of conversing with Him. God who created the universe, the God who finds nothing impossible, listens to prayer.

What will you ask God? Will you come humbly before Him with soul-deep, passionate prayer? Always remember "the effectual fervent prayer of a righteous man availeth much."

- **Based on Jeremiah 32:17[163], what is too hard for God?**

- **Read Ephesians 6:18[164], how and when are we to pray?**

> *"Do you know why I often ask Christians, 'What's the biggest thing you've asked God for this week?' I remind them that they are going to God, the Father, the Maker of the Universe. The One who holds the world in His hands. What did you ask for? Did you ask for peanuts, toys, trinkets, or did you ask for continents?"* ~ Dawson Troutman

Now how will you pray?

You have the power of Christ within you and the power to pray mighty prayers. "The effective prayer of a righteous man can accomplish much. Elijah was a man with a nature like ours, and he prayed earnestly that it would not rain, and it did not rain on the earth for three years and six months" (James 5:16-17 NASB).

- **What happened in Acts 12:5-16[165] when believers prayed for Peter?**

The power of prayer sets the prisoner free. As a follower and believer of Christ, you are given this wonderful power. Praise God, you are given a wonderful gift of praise and prayer.

I sat slumped at the kitchen table. My health had been up and down for weeks and was getting worse. Then at 9:48 that morning, I felt a surge in my spirit. I knew someone prayed for me, I knew without a doubt God had moved.

The illness, the headache that had been growing all morning was suddenly gone. I felt it lift and knew it had lifted by the hand of God, moved by someone's sweet prayers.

Thank you, dear friend, whoever you are. Thank you for being one who felt that gentle nudge to pray, who didn't ignore the prompting, but went to battle in the heavenlies on my behalf. Thank you.

A few days later, when I couldn't breathe, couldn't catch my breath when some unexpected, soul-shattering news came, I knew at 4:13 pm you prayed. Thank you.

Thank you for listening to the Holy Spirit. Thank you for praying for me. Thank you for breathing grace, giving life support when breath can't be found and when life is too hard to take a breath on my own. Thank you for praying.

Oh friends, your prayers make a difference.

Your prayers provide heavenly CPR. Your prayers are God's grace breathing into others who need life support. Your prayers are the oxygen mask for those struggling to breathe during difficult events.

Please pray when the Holy Spirit prompts you to pray. When God's spirit moves, move in action, move right then, for someone may not be able to stand and needs your prayer support. Breathe grace through your prayers, for your prayers drop mercy on those who are hurting. Please pray.

> *"Prayer for another person is like touching God with one hand and touching the person with the other. That's what intercessory prayer is all about." ~ Jim Cymbala*

During a time of prayer, I wondered, what if I expected the best from God?

What if I expected the best, because God's ways are the best, His love is the best, and He loves me the best?

I've been reading books by people who are currently living in countries where Christians are persecuted. These people have amazing faith and witness many miracles.

I wonder do they see God moving because they have no preconceived notions about what God can and cannot do?

They expect God to work in mighty ways and therefore see Him work in mighty ways.

In many areas, religion is boxed into a sanitized version of Christianity.

- **What are we told in Matthew 13:58[166]?**

If we never expect the best and believe the best, will we ever see the best? What if I lived in the holy boldness and divine confidence by remembering the greatness of my God?

What if I expected the unexpected of exceedingly, abundantly more than I could ask or imagine? Just writing those words, I can feel a holy confidence rising.

> *"In your prayers, above everything else, beware of limiting God, not only through unbelief but also by thinking you know exactly what He can do. Learn to expect the unexpected, beyond all that you ask or think." ~ Andrew Murray*

The truth is nothing is impossible for God.

God's love is unfailing, His supremacy is unstoppable, and His might is mightier than anything or anyone. As Christians, His power lives within us. The best, The Very Best, lives within us. Does my life, and do my prayers, change when I remember those facts? To be honest, yes.

Problems become smaller when situations are viewed through the lens of our great God. Dreams become bigger when we remember the might and power of our GREAT God.

Worry and hesitation ends as boldness and confidence takes over because our boldness and confidence are in our loving, unfailing, ALL-POWERFUL God.

Pray with me?

Heavenly Father, praise You! Praise You that I can come to You with my every request and need. God, I want Your best and Your perfect will. Through the hard, difficult, good, bad, and ugly, please grant me eyes to watch for how You are moving and working. Help me live in Your holy boldness and confidence. I want to see and experience the exceedingly, abundantly more than I could ask or imagine.

Praise You and thank You that nothing is too hard for You, nothing is impossible for You, for You are a GREAT God! Help me never limit You and always expect the best, for You are the BEST! Praise You Holy Father! I love You!

I ask these things in the name of Your Son, Jesus Christ, who is my Savior.

Amen!

Oh friend, pray and rest in the marvelous power of our marvelous God.

Moving on rest

Our little dog, Chipper, couldn't wait to get out and explore the world. He didn't care where he was going—he just wanted to get there as fast as possible. We tried to keep him close, but no, he thought he knew so much better. Pull ... cough ... tug ... hack ....

He pulled and the pressure continued on the collar because he was too busy sniffing, pawing, and exploring his world. Chipper had a love/hate relationship with his leash. He loved the walk but would have preferred to run free. He didn't realize his leash was not for punishment, but for safety. He didn't know which path to take, didn't know the right way to go, and that he would have had great walks without pressure if he would have just stayed close.

I've done the same things. I've complained about the unbearable pressure of life's pace, begging God to give me extra slack so I could go play on a different path. "Come on God ... pull, hack, let's go ... cough."

Thinking I knew the best plans, I've plowed ahead and then wondered why on earth were there so many struggles, problems, and difficulties. I'll admit I am a busy bee, or perhaps, a busy Buffaloe.

I keep moving forward. I want to do things for God. Stay busy for God. Do good. Be good. Be a good servant. Do lots of stuff for God. Be a good worker. Do, be, do, be, do, be, do....

My life wouldn't have been as busy, or have been as hard, if only I would have followed the Master.

Jesus said, "Follow Me" (Matthew 4:19). Following Jesus is not a straight line, He leads through mountains and valleys, through the wild, crazy, good and bad, the boring and mundane. The journey isn't only about a destination, it's about following and living in the presence of The One who longs to be present in our lives.

Jesus assures that His sheep hear His voice, and He knows them, and they follow Him (John 10:27).

Every day you live on this planet, you have purpose. God's plans are perfect, beautiful, and eternal. Keep going. You are not home yet. Listen for the voice of Jesus whispering in your soul, follow Him, love Him, obey Him, and your life will be an amazing adventure.

> *"Follow Me. Two simple words that change everything. You will never be bored. You will always have purpose. You will never lack joy. But it will cost you. ... The call to follow Jesus is not simply an invitation to pray a prayer; it's a summons to lose your life—and to find new life in him." ~ David Platt*

- **What did Jesus say in Luke 9:23[167]?**

When Jesus tells His followers to deny themselves, take up their cross and follow Him, He is offering the grand adventure of an eternal lifetime. Taking up your cross to follow Jesus is an invitation to lay down your life to pick up His resurrected, eternal life.

Because Jesus went to the cross, your sins are forgiven and happy, blessed, and fortunate is the one whose sins have been forgiven (Psalm 32:1). Because of Jesus Christ's death on the cross, those who believe in Him, turn to Him, give their lives to Him, are delivered from the power of sin and death.

Pick up your cross and follow is not an invitation for a life of drudgery, it is an invitation to a new, never-ending, amazing joy-filled life through the power, might, glory, peace, hope, encouragement, courage, comfort, compassion, kindness, unfailing love and every blessing in Jesus.

> *"When our relationship with God is passionate, the race we run becomes a 'want to' instead of a 'have to.' When you are fueled by the love and grace of God, you will have the inner strength required to keep running and not give up. Every step of your run will be part of the adventure of your love affair with Jesus."*
> *~ Christine Caine[168]*

Have you felt the urge, a nudge by the Holy Spirit, to step out in faith to do something the world thinks won't matter or is downright crazy?

- **According to 1 Corinthians 1:27-28[169] what did God choose?**

God uses the weak, the powerless, the regular people to do amazing things to show the amazing power of God.

Sometimes it seems silly to think one tiny act could result in something incredible. However, just as when dominoes are standing in a line, one push sends them in motion, so too can your one act of obedience open God's door to show His power and glory.

A step toward a burning bush, led Moses on a God-adventure of a lifetime. One small shepherd boy ignored all odds, trusted God, took down a giant and became a king. One step of faith and obedience opens the door to the next step and unlocks more faith.

> *"I am convinced that when we take a serious look at what Jesus really meant when he said, 'Follow me,' we will discover that there is far more pleasure to be experienced in him, indescribably greater power to be realized with him, and a much higher purpose to be accomplished for him than anything else this world has to offer." ~ David Platt[170]*

Don't miss the grand adventure God has planned for your life. Fame, fortune, and bright lights may not be on God's agenda; however, you can trust His plans are always the best. Keep following Jesus.

- **Read 1 Corinthians 9:24-25[171] and Philippians 3:12-14[172]. What are you supposed to do? What will you receive?**

Beyond earthly sight an eternal prize awaits. Follow Jesus, run your race, and whatever you are called to do, do it well for the glory of God.

- **Read Philippians 1:6[173]. What can you be confident in?**

- **Read the following verses and underline all the ways God will guide you.**

    "You will make known to me the path of life; in Your presence is fullness of joy; in Your right hand there are pleasures forever" (Psalm 16:11 NASB).

    "I will instruct you and teach you in the way you should go; I will counsel you with my loving eye upon you" (Psalm 32:8 NIV).

    "For You are my rock and my fortress; for Your name's sake You will lead me and guide me" (Psalm 31:3 NASB).

    "Your word is a lamp to my feet and a light to my path" (Psalm 119:105 NASB).

    "When you walk about, they will guide you; when you sleep, they will watch over you; and when you awake, they will talk to you" (Proverbs 6:22 NASB).

    "He restores my soul; He guides me in the paths of righteousness for His name's sake" (Psalm 23:3 NASB).

    "With Your counsel You will guide me, and afterward receive me to glory" (Psalm 73:24 NASB).

> "Your ears will hear a word behind you, 'This is the way, walk in it,' whenever you turn to the right or to the left" (Isaiah 30:21 NASB).

Whatever God calls you to do, God will show you the way and help you complete the task.

Cliff Young grew up on his family farm of approximately 2000 acres. During the depression, Cliff's family couldn't afford horses, so he would run on foot to manage their herd of almost 2000 sheep.

In 1983, at the age of sixty-one, Cliff decided to run a 544-mile race in Australia. Leaving his dentures behind because they rattled, he came to the starting line in overalls and work boots.

Cliff ran a slow, loping pace and trailed the large pack of other runners. When the other competitors stopped to sleep, Cliff kept running.

He kept going, imagining a storm was coming and he was running after his sheep. He ran continuously for five days, fifteen hours and four minutes. Cliff won the race over the other competitors by ten hours.

Cliff didn't even know a $10,000 prize waited for the winner. He felt bad accepting the money since he believed the other five who finished worked as hard as he. So, he split the money equally among the others and kept none for himself.

Cliff ran to win. He kept running. No matter how tired he was, or how long the journey, he kept moving forward. He kept his eyes on the finish, he finished strong, and he shared the joy with others.

You don't have to be the fastest, have the latest accessories, be the youngest, or even the most qualified to win your race. No one else is like you, no one can run your race but you. You are qualified to finish in the qualification of Christ. Jesus finished his earthly race to help you through every earthly challenge and bring you safely home.

Hebrews 11 is called the Hall of Faith chapter listing many of the heroes of the Christian faith. The author lists imperfect men and women who ran their race for God, completing the tasks they were given, and keeping their eyes on a heavenly reward.

- **Read Hebrews 12:1-2[174]. What are we told to do?**

Your journey is cheered on in heaven. Your faithfulness to Christ noted by others and noted in heaven. Trust God to help you run your race. Obey God and trust Him to guide you.

Jesus said, "If anyone loves Me, he will keep My word; and My Father will love him, and We will come to him and make Our home with him" (John 14:23 NKJV).

Follow Jesus. Trust Jesus, trust His love, trust that He will lead you safely through this life into the next.

Several years ago, we watched two videos made by a soft drink company with race driver, Jeff Gordon. Jeff, disguised as an older gentleman, visited a car dealership, and took an unsuspecting car salesman on the test drive of his life.

The poor car salesman was terrified, horrified, and screamed during much of the wild, fast speed "test" drive.

By the time Jeff pulled back in the sales lot, the salesman jumped out of the car ready to call the police.

However, when Jeff identified himself, the man's face showed relief, then delight. And he immediately asked Jeff, "Want to do it again?"

Once the video went viral, several journalists claimed the video was a fake. The soft drink company and Jeff again teamed up.

Disguised as a cab driver, Jeff picked up one of the automotive journalists who had questioned the authenticity of the original video. The man thought he was going to the airport. Instead, Jeff took the man on a hair-raising, crazy ride. The journalist screamed, kicked, and begged to get out.

Yet, when Jeff came to a stop and identified himself, the man wanted to go for another ride.

The thing that struck me was, how many times do we beg, scream, curse, and demand to get out of difficult situations -- even though God is in control, even though The One who loves us best, who will never fail us or forsake us, is in control. What if we truly realized this fact and enjoyed the ride?

What if we remembered (never forgot) that God is with us, and His power, wisdom, and strength are in the driver's seat?

What if we joyfully buckled in knowing that each trial, each wild ride, results in more strength, power, and knowledge that God is in control, and our faith is growing stronger. Let's do it again, let's trust God to drive us safely home.

Rest easy, friends. God loves you and will guide you safely home.

*I have loved you with an everlasting love.
Come to Me, all you who labor and are heavy-laden and overburdened, and I will cause you to rest. I will ease and relieve and refresh your souls. Take My yoke upon you and learn of Me, for I am gentle (meek) and humble (lowly) in heart, and you will find rest (relief and ease and refreshment and recreation and blessed quiet) for your souls (Jeremiah 31:3, Matthew 11:28-29).*

Appendix: Information about Jesus and Heaven

There's an old joke about two hunters in the woods being chased by a bear. One hunter yells out to the other as he runs past, "I don't have to be faster than the bear, I just have to beat you!" Unfortunately, many people think the same is true about gaining entrance to heaven. Just do better than the others, be good and it will all work out fine.

The problem this presents is:

>Who says how much goodness is required?
>Who is keeping score?
>And at any given moment, how can I know where I stand?

Does that mean as long as someone is better than Adolf Hitler or Attila the Hun they've got a shot? But what if someone has to be as good as a Mother Theresa? Okay, maybe the chances aren't as good.

The Bible goes to the real issue with God and sets it straight for us. None of us deserves to go to heaven because everyone has sinned. We've all thought bad things or done bad things. Romans 3:23 says, "Everyone has sinned. No one measures up to God's glory." We tend to rank sins, but God says sin is sin and there is no way through our own "goodness" we can ever stand in front of a Holy and pure God.

Sometimes that doesn't sound fair, don't all the "good" people deserve to go to heaven? Then again who defines fair and what makes one deserving? Even Jesus said no one is good except God alone (Mark 10:18).

Think about this...the designer and creator of the universe (God) also made the rules and the way for salvation, for those to come to heaven. God knew people would sin, and no matter how hard they tried they would never reach perfection. Sure, we can be pretty good, but our being good doesn't result in purity and holiness. With God it's not just how bad we are, it's how good we're not.

However, I have wonderful news! God, because of His great love, God gave His one and only Son, Jesus Christ, so that whoever believes in Him will not perish, but have eternal life (John 3:16). Jesus came to give us life in abundance (John 10:10).

Jesus, His only Son (God in the flesh), willingly sacrificed His life through dying on the cross to make the way clear for us to get to our heavenly home. Three days after the death of Jesus Christ on a cross, He rose from the grave. Because Jesus triumphed over death, hell, and the grave, He held the keys to eternal life. He said, "I am the way and the truth and the life. No one comes to the Father except through me" (John 14:6).

Good works, church membership, denominations, religiosity, good family history, etc. won't get you into heaven. Even saying you believe in God isn't enough.

The Bible says, "You believe that there is one God. Good! Even the demons believe that—and shudder" (James 2:19). Even the demons believe God exists.

Christ Jesus did something that we could not do for ourselves.

We cannot measure up, but we can give up our lives to Jesus Christ, and when we do, His cross bridges the gap, the door is opened, and we can stand clothed in the Holy righteousness of Jesus Christ. Only through the death and resurrection of Jesus can the door be opened for forgiveness and eternal life. "I am the door, and the person who enters through me will be saved..." (John 10:9). Salvation can't be earned, only through faith in God's Son, Jesus Christ does the door to heaven open.

Jesus said, "Here I am! I stand at the door and knock. If anyone hears my voice and opens the door, I will come in and eat with him, and he with me" (Revelation 3:20). Jesus has opened the door and your goodness isn't the issue.

Once you repent of your sins and ask Him to be your Lord and Savior, Repentance is not just an acknowledgement of sin, but a turning away from sin. Jesus works in you to help and free you from the bondage of sin.

The Bible tells us that if we confess our sins, God is faithful and just to forgive us and cleanse us from all wickedness. (1 John 1:9). There is forgiveness of sins for all who repent. (Luke 24:47)

Why is it so easy? Because God is good, God is love, and God wants nothing more than for you to come home to the heaven He created for His beautiful but marred creation.

What do you do? The apostle Paul put it pretty plainly, "If you confess with your mouth, 'Jesus is Lord,' and believe in your heart that God raised him from the dead, you will be saved. For it is with your heart that you believe and are justified, and it is with your mouth that you confess and are saved" (Romans 10:9-10).

On the following page is a simple example prayer.

"Lord Jesus, I'm the sinner You came to save and I need You. Thank You for dying on the cross for my sins. I open the door of my life and receive You as my Savior and Lord. Thank You for forgiving my sins and giving me eternal life. Please take control of my life and make me the kind of person You want me to be." In the name of Jesus, Amen.

Being a Christian is more than just saying a prayer, true Christianity is life-changing and life-altering. A personal relationship with Jesus Christ is a spark that cannot be extinguished, a safe harbor in the storms of life, hope and peace that never ends, joy midst sorrow, and life everlasting.

Please find a good Bible-teaching church, and when you feel it's time, talk to your pastor about being baptized. Begin to share with others what has taken place in your life. Take time to pray (talking with God). God, who made you, longs to be with you for now and forever.

With Christ in your heart and life, you will be blessed with heaven. Heaven won't be a place to sit around with little angel wings bored to tears and playing harps. Heaven is a vibrant, exciting, peaceful, ecstatic place of fellowship, love, and never-ending joy.

One day we'll arrive at our heavenly home and all our hardships and difficulties will make sense. We'll see the big picture – the lives we touched along the way, the people we helped, and the ones that helped us. We'll see the times we were saved from greater disaster, and we'll embrace those who wait for our homecoming.

Please come home to heaven.

Anyone who trusts in Jesus "will never be disappointed.' That Scripture says 'anyone' because there is no difference between those who are Jews and those who are not. The same Lord is the Lord of all and gives many blessings to all who trust in him, as the Scripture says, 'Anyone who calls on the Lord will be saved'" (Romans 10:11-13 NCV).

"I have loved you with an everlasting love; I have drawn you with loving-kindness. As the Father has loved me, so have I loved you. For as high as the heavens are above the earth, so great is his love for those who fear him. Long before he laid down earth's foundations, he had us in mind, had settled on us as the focus of his love, to be made whole and holy by his love. Long, long ago he decided to adopt us into his family through Jesus Christ. (What pleasure he took in planning this!) He wanted us to enter into the celebration of his lavish gift-giving by the hand of his beloved Son. It's in Christ that we find out who we are and what we are living for. Long before we first heard of Christ and got our hopes up, he had his eye on us, had designs on us for glorious living, part of the overall purpose he is working out in everything and everyone. If anyone is in Christ, he is a new creature; the old things passed away; behold, new things have come" (John 15:9 NIV, Jeremiah 31:3 NIV, Psalm 103:11 NIV, Ephesians 1:3-6, 11-12 MSG, 2 Corinthians 5:17 NASB).

"God will wipe away every tear from their eyes; there shall be no more death, nor sorrow, nor crying. There shall be no more pain, for the former things have passed away. Then He who sat on the throne said, 'Behold, I make all things new.' ... I am the Alpha and the Omega, the Beginning and the End. I will give of the fountain of the water of life freely to him who thirsts. He who overcomes shall inherit all things, and I will be his God and he shall be My son" (Revelation 21:4-7 NKJV).

About the Author

Lisa Buffaloe is a happily married mom, author, and speaker. When she's not writing, she enjoys working in her yard, exploring God's beautiful nature, and taking long walks with her sweet husband.

Lisa loves sharing God's unending love and that through Him we find healing, restoration, renewal, and joy.

Visit Lisa at https://lisabuffaloe.com

Books by Lisa Buffaloe
(Updated July 2023)

Fiction
The Masterpiece Beneath
Nadia's Hope (Hope and Grace Series, Book 1)
  Prodigal Nights (Hope and Grace Series, 2)
  Writing Her Heart (Hope and Grace Series, 3)
  The Discovery Chapter (Hope and Grace Series, 4)
  Open Lens (Hope and Grace Series, 5)
The Fortune
Grace for the Char-Baked

Non-Fiction
Float by Faith
Heart and Soul Medication
Time with The Timeless One
The Forgotten Resting Place
Present in His Presence
We Were Meant for Paradise
One Lit Step: Devotions for your journey
The Unnamed Devotional
Flying on His Wings
Unfailing Treasures
No Wound Too Deep for The Deep Love of Christ
Living Joyfully Free Devotional, (Volume 1)
Living Joyfully Free Devotional, (Volume 2)

Acknowledgements

Thank you, Jesus for setting me free and healing the broken places in my soul. Thank you for your grace and mercy. Thank you for loving me. I'm eternally grateful for your unfailing love. Thank you that I can rest forever in you. Thank you, thank you, thank you!

Thank you, Dennis Buffaloe for blessing me as your wife. I am so grateful God brought us together and gifted me with you. Thank you for loving me and giving me a safe place to heal, grow, and write. Thank you for your continued support and love for me and our sweet son. I love you so very much!

Thank you, Tammy Harvey for the grammar edit. You are a blessing! Thank you, Sara Butler, Cathy Morningstar Brewer, and Cheri Broadfoot for your feedback and encouragement during the process of writing. Thank you all!

A big thank you to my family, friends (online and in person), and readers who have encouraged me throughout the writing process. Thank you for your support and love. Thank you!

Bible credits

The original text of the Bible is rich and full, written in Hebrew, Aramaic, and Greek. The various Bible versions I use during writing are to share the one most appropriate to reveal the beauty and truth of each verse.

Any highlights or underlining on scripture have been added by me. I will use several verses many times so that those wonderful, restful truths will steep deep in your soul.

I gratefully thank each Bible publisher for the use of the scripture quotations.

Scripture taken from the New Century Version® (NCV). Copyright © 2005 by Thomas Nelson, Inc. Used by permission. All rights reserved.

Living Bible (TLB) The Living Bible copyright © 1971 by Tyndale House Foundation. Used by permission of Tyndale House Publishers Inc., Carol Stream, Illinois 60188. All rights reserved.

Scripture quotations taken from the New American Standard Bible®(NASB), Copyright © 1960, 1962, 1963, 1968, 1971, 1972, 1973, 1975, 1977, 1995 by The Lockman Foundation Used by permission. www.Lockman.org

Scripture quotations marked (NLT) are taken from the Holy Bible, New Living Translation, copyright © 1996, 2004, 2007 by Tyndale House Foundation. Used by permission of Tyndale House Publishers, Inc., Carol Stream, Illinois 60188. All rights reserved.

THE HOLY BIBLE, NEW INTERNATIONAL VERSION®, NIV® Copyright © 1973, 1978, 1984, 2011 by Biblica, Inc.™ Used by permission. All rights reserved worldwide.

NET Bible® copyright ©1996-2006 by Biblical Studies Press, L.L.C. http://netbible.com

Scripture taken from the New King James Version®. Copyright © 1982 by Thomas Nelson, Inc. Used by permission. All rights reserved.

The ESV® Bible (The Holy Bible, English Standard Version®). ESV® Text Edition: 2016. Copyright © 2001 by Crossway, a publishing ministry of Good News Publishers. The ESV® text has been reproduced in cooperation with and by permission of Good News Publishers. Unauthorized reproduction of this publication is prohibited. All rights reserved.

Scripture taken from *The Message*. Copyright © 1993, 1994, 1995, 1996, 2000, 2001, 2002. Used by permission of NavPress Publishing Group.

Scripture quotations taken from the New Life Version (NLV) Copyright © 1969–2003 by Christian Literature International, P.O. Box 777, Canby, OR 97013. Used by permission.

Scripture quotations taken from the Amplified® Bible (AMP), Copyright © 2015 by The Lockman Foundation Used by permission. www.Lockman.org

Scripture quotations taken from the Amplified® Bible (AMPC), Copyright © 1954, 1958, 1962, 1964, 1965, 1987 by The Lockman Foundation Used by permission. www.Lockman.org

Holman Christian Standard Bible (HCSB) Copyright © 1999, 2000, 2002, 2003, 2009 by Holman Bible Publishers, Nashville Tennessee. All rights reserved.

Footnotes and Scripture

---

1 Story by Greg Lucas
   http://sheepdogger.blogspot.com/2013/08/indispensable.html?m=1

2 1 John 4:15-18 (NASB) "Whoever confesses that Jesus is the Son of God, God abides in him, and he in God. We have come to know and have believed the love which God has for us. God is love, and the one who abides in love abides in God, and God abides in him. By this, love is perfected with us, so that we may have confidence in the day of judgment; because as He is, so also are we in this world. There is no fear in love; but perfect love casts out fear, because fear involves punishment, and the one who fears is not perfected in love."

3 Psalm 139:17-18 (NASB) "How precious also are Your thoughts to me, O God! How vast is the sum of them! If I should count them, they would outnumber the sand. When I awake, I am still with You."

4 Psalm 121:1-4 (NASB) I will lift up my eyes to the mountains; from where shall my help come? My help comes from the Lord, Who made heaven and earth. He will not allow your foot to slip; He who keeps you will not slumber. Behold, He who keeps Israel will neither slumber nor sleep.

5 Zephaniah 3:17 (NKJV) "The Lord your God in your midst, the Mighty One, will save; He will rejoice over you with gladness, He will quiet you with His love, He will rejoice over you with singing."

6 Matthew 10:30 (NKJV) "the very hairs of your head are all numbered."

7 Isaiah 49:15-16 (NASB) "Can a woman forget her nursing child and have no compassion on the son of her womb? Even these may forget, but I will not forget you. Behold, I have inscribed you on the palms of My hands..."

8 1 Corinthians 13:4-8 (NASB) Love is patient, love is kind and is not jealous; love does not brag and is not arrogant, does not act unbecomingly; it does not seek its own, is not provoked, does not take into account a wrong suffered, does not rejoice in unrighteousness, but rejoices with the truth; bears all things, believes all things, hopes all things, endures all things. Love never fails"

9 Matthew 25:14-29 (NASB) "For it is just like a man about to go on a journey, who called his own slaves and entrusted his possessions to them. To one he gave five talents, to another, two, and to another, one, each according to his own ability; and he went on his journey. Immediately the one who had received the five talents went and traded with them, and gained five more talents. In the same manner the one who had received the two talents gained two more. But he who received the one talent went away, and dug a hole in the ground and hid his master's money. Now after a long time the master of those

slaves came and settled accounts with them. The one who had received the five talents came up and brought five more talents, saying, 'Master, you entrusted five talents to me. See, I have gained five more talents.' His master said to him, 'Well done, good and faithful slave. You were faithful with a few things, I will put you in charge of many things; enter into the joy of your master.' Also the one who had received the two talents came up and said, 'Master, you entrusted two talents to me. See, I have gained two more talents.' His master said to him, 'Well done, good and faithful slave. You were faithful with a few things, I will put you in charge of many things; enter into the joy of your master.' And the one also who had received the one talent came up and said, 'Master, I knew you to be a hard man, reaping where you did not sow and gathering where you scattered no seed. And I was afraid, and went away and hid your talent in the ground. See, you have what is yours.' But his master answered and said to him, 'You wicked, lazy slave, you knew that I reap where I did not sow and gather where I scattered no seed. Then you ought to have put my money in the bank, and on my arrival I would have received my money back with interest. Therefore take away the talent from him, and give it to the one who has the ten talents.' For to everyone who has, more shall be given, and he will have an abundance; but from the one who does not have, even what he does have shall be taken away."

10 Isaiah 41:10 (NASB) "Do not fear, for I am with you; do not anxiously look about you, for I am your God. I will strengthen you, surely I will help you, surely I will uphold you with My righteous right hand."

11 Isaiah 41:13 (NASB) "For I am the Lord your God, who upholds your right hand, Who says to you, 'Do not fear, I will help you.'"

12 Psalm 94:18 (NKJV) "If I say, 'My foot slips,' Your mercy, O LORD, will hold me up."

13 Luke 15:11-20 (NET Bible) Then Jesus said, "A man had two sons. The younger of them said to his father, 'Father, give me the share of the estate that will belong to me.' So he divided his assets between them. After a few days, the younger son gathered together all he had and left on a journey to a distant country, and there he squandered his wealth with a wild lifestyle. Then after he had spent everything, a severe famine took place in that country, and he began to be in need. So he went and worked for one of the citizens of that country, who sent him to his fields to feed pigs. He was longing to eat the carob pods the pigs were eating, but no one gave him anything. But when he came to his senses he said, 'How many of my father's hired workers have food enough to spare, but here I am dying from hunger! I will get up and go to my father and say to him, 'Father, I have sinned against heaven and against you. I am no longer worthy to be called your son; treat me like one of your hired workers.' So he got up and went to his father. But while he was still a long way from home his father saw him, and his heart went out to him; he ran and hugged his son and kissed him."

14 Psalm 37:23-24 (NASB) "The steps of a man are established by the Lord, and He delights in his way. When he falls, he will not be hurled headlong, because the Lord is the One who holds his hand."

15 2 Corinthians 1:3-5 (NASB) "Blessed be the God and Father of our Lord Jesus Christ, the Father of mercies and God of all comfort, who comforts us in all our affliction so that

we will be able to comfort those who are in any affliction with the comfort with which we ourselves are comforted by God. For just as the sufferings of Christ are ours in abundance, so also our comfort is abundant through Christ."

16 Isaiah 54:10 (NASB) "For the mountains may be removed and the hills may shake, but My lovingkindness will not be removed from you, and My covenant of peace will not be shaken, says the Lord who has compassion on you."

17 Psalm 91 (NASB) "He who dwells in the shelter of the Most High will abide in the shadow of the Almighty. I will say to the LORD, 'My refuge and my fortress, My God, in whom I trust!' For it is He who delivers you from the snare of the trapper and from the deadly pestilence. He will cover you with His pinions, and under His wings you may seek refuge; His faithfulness is a shield and bulwark. You will not be afraid of the terror by night, or of the arrow that flies by day; of the pestilence that stalks in darkness, or of the destruction that lays waste at noon. A thousand may fall at your side and ten thousand at your right hand, but it shall not approach you. You will only look on with your eyes and see the recompense of the wicked. For you have made the LORD, my refuge, even the Most High, your dwelling place. No evil will befall you, nor will any plague come near your tent. For He will give His angels charge concerning you, to guard you in all your ways. They will bear you up in their hands, that you do not strike your foot against a stone. You will tread upon the lion and cobra, the young lion and the serpent you will trample down. Because he has loved Me, therefore I will deliver him; I will set him securely on high, because he has known My name. He will call upon Me, and I will answer him; I will be with him in trouble; I will rescue him and honor him. With a long life I will satisfy him and let him see My salvation."

18 1 Corinthians 1:9 (NKJV) "God is faithful, by whom you were called into the fellowship of His Son, Jesus Christ our Lord."

19 Genesis 5:24 (AMPC) "Enoch walked [in habitual fellowship] with God; and he was not, for God took him [home with Him]."

20 Psalm 139:2 (NASB) "You know when I sit down and when I rise up; You understand my thought from afar."

21 Jeremiah 33:3 (NIV) "Call to Me and I will answer you and tell you great and unsearchable things you do not know."

22 John 10:27 (NASB) "My sheep hear my voice and I know them and they follow Me."

23 Ephesians 2:10 (NLT) "For we are God's masterpiece. He has created us anew in Christ Jesus, so we can do the good things he planned for us long ago."

24 Revelation 3:20 (NLT) "Look! I stand at the door and knock. If you hear my voice and open the door, I will come in, and we will share a meal together as friends."
25 Deuteronomy 31:8 (NKJV) "And the Lord, He is the One who goes before you. He will be with you, He will not leave you nor forsake you; do not fear nor be dismayed."

26 Isaiah 43:1-3a (NASB) "But now, thus says the LORD, your Creator, O Jacob, and He who formed you, O Israel, 'Do not fear, for I have redeemed you; I have called you by name; you are Mine! When you pass through the waters, I will be with you; and through the rivers, they will not overflow you. when you walk through the fire, you will not be scorched, nor will the flame burn you. For I am the LORD your God"

27 Psalm 33:18 (NIV) "...the eyes of the Lord are on those who fear him, on those whose hope is in his unfailing love."

28 Matthew 28:20 (NASB) "... I am with you always, even to the end of the age."

29 Romans 8:38-39 (NASB) "For I am convinced that neither death, nor life, nor angels, nor principalities, nor things present, nor things to come, nor powers, nor height, nor depth, nor any other created thing, will be able to separate us from the love of God, which is in Christ Jesus our Lord."

30 Romans 8:28 (AMP) "And we know [with great confidence] that God [who is deeply concerned about us] causes all things to work together [as a plan] for good for those who love God, to those who are called according to His plan and purpose."

31 Luke 1:37 (KJV) "For with God nothing shall be impossible.."

32 Romans 3:23 (NKJV) "all have sinned and fall short of the glory of God."

33 Romans 5:8 (NLT) "But God showed his great love for us by sending Christ to die for us while we were still sinners."

34 Philippians 4:19 (NKJV) "And my God shall supply all your need according to His riches in glory by Christ Jesus."

35 Hebrews 4:15-16 (AMPC) "For we do not have a High Priest Who is unable to understand and sympathize and have a shared feeling with our weaknesses and infirmities and liability to the assaults of temptation, but One Who has been tempted in every respect as we are, yet without sinning. Let us then fearlessly and confidently and boldly draw near to the throne of grace (the throne of God's unmerited favor to us sinners), that we may receive mercy [for our failures] and find grace to help in good time for every need [appropriate help and well-timed help, coming just when we need it]."

36 John 21:20 (AMP) "Peter turned and saw the disciple whom Jesus loved following them; the one who also had leaned back on His chest at the supper..."

37 Romans 8:14-17 (AMP) "For all who are allowing themselves to be led by the Spirit of God are sons of God. For you have not received a spirit of slavery leading again to fear [of God's judgment], but you have received the Spirit of adoption as sons [the Spirit producing sonship] by which we [joyfully] cry, 'Abba! Father!' The Spirit Himself testifies and confirms together with our spirit [assuring us] that we [believers] are children of God. And if [we are His] children, [then we are His] heirs also: heirs of God and fellow heirs

with Christ [sharing His spiritual blessing and inheritance], if indeed we share in His suffering so that we may also share in His glory."

38 John 15:15 (NIV) "I no longer call you servants, because a servant does not know his master's business. Instead, I have called you friends, for everything that I learned from my Father I have made known to you."

39 Cowman, L. B., *Springs in the Valley*, Michigan: Zondervan, 2016

40 Matthew 11:28 (AMPC) Jesus said, "Come to Me, all you who labor and are heavy-laden and overburdened, and I will cause you to rest. [I will ease and relieve and refresh your souls.]"

41 Mark 6:31 (NKJV "Come aside by yourselves to a deserted place and rest a while...."

42 Matthew 11:28-30 (NASB) "Come to Me, all who are weary and heavy-laden, and I will give you rest. Take My yoke upon you and learn from Me, for I am gentle and humble in heart, and you will find rest for your souls. For My yoke is easy and My burden is light."

43 John 15:11 (AMPC) "I have told you these things, that My joy and delight may be in you, and that your joy and gladness may be of full measure and complete and overflowing."

44 Ephesians 2:8 (NET Bible) "For by grace you are saved through faith, and this is not from yourselves, it is the gift of God."

45 Luke 23:33-34 (NASB) "When they came to the place called The Skull, there they crucified Him and the criminals, one on the right and the other on the left. But Jesus was saying,'Father, forgive them; for they do not know what they are doing.'"

46 Matthew 6:14-15 (NLT) "If you forgive those who sin against you, your heavenly Father will forgive you. But if you refuse to forgive others, your Father will not forgive your sins."

47 Buchanan, Mark. *Hidden in Plain Sight: The Secret of More*, Tennessee: Thomas Nelson, 2007

48 Proverbs 15:3 (NASB) "The eyes of the Lord are in every place, watching the evil and the good."

49 Matthew 10:26 (NASB) "Therefore do not fear them, for there is nothing concealed that will not be revealed, or hidden that will not be known.

50 Isaiah 13:11 (NLT) "I, the Lord, will punish the world for its evil and the wicked for their sin. I will crush the arrogance of the proud and humble the pride of the mighty."

51 Ephesians 4:26 (AMPC), Ephesians 4:27 (AMP) "When angry, do not sin; do not ever let your wrath (your exasperation, your fury or indignation) last until the sun goes down.

And do not give the devil an opportunity [to lead you into sin by holding a grudge, or nurturing anger, or harboring resentment, or cultivating bitterness]."

52 Acts 13:22 (NASB) "...He raised up David to be their king, concerning whom He also testified and said, 'I have found David the son of Jesse, a man after My heart, who will do all My will.'"

53 Exodus 33:11 (NASB) "Thus the Lord used to speak to Moses face to face, just as a man speaks to his friend...."

54 Matthew 1:5-17 (NASB) "Salmon was the father of Boaz by Rahab, Boaz was the father of Obed by Ruth, and Obed the father of Jesse. Jesse was the father of David the king. David was the father of Solomon ...Jacob was the father of Joseph the husband of Mary, by whom Jesus was born, who is called the Messiah. So all the generations from Abraham to David are fourteen generations; ... to the Messiah, fourteen generations."

55 John 8:7 (NASB) "But when they persisted in asking Him, He straightened up, and said to them, 'He who is without sin among you, let him be the first to throw a stone at her.'"

56 Luke 4:18 (NASB) "The Spirit of the Lord is upon Me, because He anointed Me to preach the gospel to the poor. He has sent Me to proclaim release to the captives, and recovery of sight to the blind, to set free those who are oppressed."

57 1 John 1:9 (NASB) "If we confess our sins, He is faithful and righteous to forgive us our sins and to cleanse us from all unrighteousness."

58 1 John 3:2-3 (NASB) "Beloved, now we are children of God, and it has not appeared as yet what we will be. We know that when He appears, we will be like Him, because we will see Him just as He is. And everyone who has this hope fixed on Him purifies himself, just as He is pure."

59 Isaiah 1:18 (NKJV) "'Come now, and let us reason together,' says the Lord, 'though your sins are like scarlet, they shall be as white as snow; though they are red like crimson, they shall be as wool."

60 2 Corinthians 5:17 (NLT) "This means that anyone who belongs to Christ has become a new person. The old life is gone; a new life has begun!"

61 Psalm 103:12 (NASB) "As far as the east is from the west, so far has He removed our transgressions from us."

62 Psalm 146:7 (NIV) "He upholds the cause of the oppressed and gives food to the hungry. The Lord sets prisoners free."

63 Romans 12:19 (NIV) "Do not take revenge, my dear friends, but leave room for God's wrath, for it is written: 'It is mine to avenge; I will repay,' says the Lord."

64 Psalm 29:11 (NCV)"The Lord gives strength to His people; the Lord blesses His people with peace."

65 Philippians 4:13 (AMP) "I can do all things [which He has called me to do] through Him who strengthens and empowers me [to fulfill His purpose—I am self-sufficient in Christ's sufficiency; I am ready for anything and equal to anything through Him who infuses me with inner strength and confident peace.]"

66 John 14:27 (NIV) "Peace I leave with you; my peace I give you. I do not give to you as the world gives. Do not let your hearts be troubled and do not be afraid."

67 Psalm 56:8 (NASB) "You have taken account of my wanderings; put my tears in Your bottle; are they not in Your book?"

68 Isaiah 43:19 (NASB) "Behold, I will do something new, now it will spring forth; will you not be aware of it? I will even make a roadway in the wilderness, rivers in the desert.:

69 Blackaby, Henry and Richard Blackaby. *Being Still with God Every Day*, Tennessee: Thomas Nelson, 2007

70 Cowman, L. B. *Streams in the Desert*, Michigan: Zondervan, 1997

71 Psalm 147:3 (AMP) God "heals the brokenhearted and binds up their wounds [healing their pain and comforting their sorrow].

72 Malachi 4:2 (NASB) "But for you who fear My name, the sun of righteousness will rise with healing in its wings; and you will go forth and skip about like calves from the stall."

73 Genesis 50:20 (NKJV) "But as for you, you meant evil against me; but God meant it for good, in order to bring it about as it is this day, to save many people alive."

74 Revelation 12:11 (NKJV) "And they overcame him by the blood of the Lamb and by the word of their testimony, and they did not love their lives to the death."

75 Philippians 3:13-14 (NIV) "Brothers and sisters, I do not consider myself yet to have taken hold of it. But one thing I do: Forgetting what is behind and straining toward what is ahead, I press on toward the goal to win the prize for which God has called me heavenward in Christ Jesus."

76 Ann Voskamp is found at www.AnnVoskamp.com. Quote used with her gracious permission.

77 Cymbala, Jim. *Fresh Faith*, Michigan: Zondervan, 1999

78 James 4:7 "Resist the devil and he will flee from you."

79 2 Corinthians 10:3-5 (NASB) "For though we walk in the flesh, we do not war according to the flesh, for the weapons of our warfare are not of the flesh, but divinely

powerful for the destruction of fortresses. We are destroying speculations and every lofty thing raised up against the knowledge of God, and we are taking every thought captive to the obedience of Christ."

80 1 Corinthians 2:16 (NASB) "For who has known the mind of the Lord, that he will instruct Him? But we have the mind of Christ."

81 Philippians 4:6-7 (AMPC) "Do not fret or have any anxiety about anything, but in every circumstance and in everything, by prayer and petition (definite requests), with thanksgiving, continue to make your wants known to God. And God's peace [shall be yours, that tranquil state of a soul assured of its salvation through Christ, and so fearing nothing from God and being content with its earthly lot of whatever sort that is, that peace] which transcends all understanding shall garrison and mount guard over your hearts and minds in Christ Jesus."

82 Psalm 104:34 (NLT) "May all my thoughts be pleasing to Him, for I rejoice in the Lord."

83 1 Peter 5:8 (NKJV) "Be sober, be vigilant; because your adversary the devil walks about like a roaring lion, seeking whom he may devour."

84 John 10:10 (NKJV) "The thief does not come except to steal, and to kill, and to destroy. I have come that they may have life, and that they may have it more abundantly."

85 Isaiah 43:18-19 (NCV) "The Lord says, 'Forget what happened before, and do not think about the past Look at the new thing I am going to do. It is already happening. Don't you see it? I will make a road in the desert and rivers in the dry land."

86 John 8:31-32 (NASB) Jesus said, "If you continue in My word, then you are truly disciples of Mine; and you will know the truth, and the truth will make you free."

87 Luke 21:15 (AMPC) "For I [Myself] will give you a mouth and such utterance and wisdom that all of your foes combined will be unable to stand against or refute."

88 Anderson, Neil T., *The Bondage Breaker*, Oregon: Harvest House Publishers, 2000

89 Luke 4:18-19 (NASB) "The Spirit of the Lord is upon Me, because He anointed Me to preach the gospel to the poor. He has sent Me to proclaim release to the captives, and recovery of sight to the blind, to set free those who are oppressed, to proclaim the favorable year of the Lord." John 8:36 (NASB) "So if the Son makes you free, you will be free indeed."

90 Exodus 14:13-30 (NASB) "Moses said to the people, 'Do not fear! Stand by and see the salvation of the Lordwhich He will accomplish for you today; for the Egyptians whom you have seen today, you will never see them again forever. The Lord will fight for you while you keep silent.' Then the Lord said to Moses, 'Why are you crying out to Me? Tell the sons of Israel to go forward. As for you, lift up your staff and stretch out your hand over the sea and divide it, and the sons of Israel shall go through the midst of the sea on dry land.' ... Then Moses stretched out his hand over the sea; and the Lord swept the sea

back by a strong east wind all night and turned the sea into dry land, so the waters were divided. The sons of Israel went through the midst of the sea on the dry land, and the waters were like a wall to them on their right hand and on their left. ...Then the Egyptians took up the pursuit, and all Pharaoh's horses, his chariots and his horsemen went in after them into the midst of the sea. ... the Lord overthrew the Egyptians in the midst of the sea. The waters returned and covered the chariots and the horsemen, even Pharaoh's entire army that had gone into the sea after them; not even one of them remained.... Thus the Lord saved Israel that day from the hand of the Egyptians, and Israel saw the Egyptians dead on the seashore."

91 Joshua 3:15-17 (NASB) "when those who carried the ark came into the Jordan, and the feet of the priests carrying the ark were dipped in the edge of the water (for the Jordan overflows all its banks all the days of harvest), the waters which were flowing down from above stood and rose up in one heap, ... So the people crossed opposite Jericho. And the priests who carried the ark of the covenant of the Lord stood firm on dry ground in the middle of the Jordan while all Israel crossed on dry ground, until all the nation had finished crossing the Jordan."

92 Joshua 6:20 (NASB) "the people shouted, and priests blew the trumpets; and when the people heard the sound of the trumpet, the people shouted with a great shout and the wall fell down flat, so that the people went up into the city, every man straight ahead, and they took the city.

93 Matthew 19:26 (NASB) "And looking at them Jesus said to them, 'With people this is impossible, but with God all things are possible.'"

94 Daniel 3:21-24 (NASB) "Then these men were tied up in their trousers, their coats, their caps and their other clothes, and were cast into the midst of the furnace of blazing fire ...Then Nebuchadnezzar the king was astounded and stood up in haste; he said to his high officials, 'Was it not three men we cast bound into the midst of the fire?' They replied to the king, 'Certainly, O king.' He said, 'Look! I see four men loosed and walking about in the midst of the fire without harm, and the appearance of the fourth is like a son of the gods!' ...Shadrach, Meshach and Abed-nego came out of the midst of the fire. ... the fire had no effect on the bodies of these men nor was the hair of their head singed, nor were their trousers damaged, nor had the smell of fire even come upon them."

95 Ephesians 3:17-19 (NET Bible) "that Christ may dwell in your hearts through faith, so that, because you have been rooted and grounded in love, you may be able to comprehend with all the saints what is the breadth and length and height and depth, and thus to know the love of Christ that surpasses knowledge, so that you may be filled up to all the fullness of God."

96 Chambers, Oswald. *My Utmost for His Highest*, Ohio: Discovery House books, Barbour Publishing, 1992

97 Isaiah 41:10 (NASB) "Do not fear, for I am with you; do not anxiously look about you, for I am your God. I will strengthen you, surely I will help you, surely I will uphold you with My righteous right hand."

98 Isaiah 26:3 (NCV) "You, Lord, give true peace to those who depend on you, because they trust you."

99 Psalm 27:5 (NLV) "For in the day of trouble He will keep me safe in His holy tent. In the secret place of His tent He will hide me. He will set me high upon a rock."

100 Psalm 4:8 (AMP) "In peace [and with a tranquil heart] I will both lie down and sleep, for You alone, O Lord, make me dwell in safety and confident trust."

101 Isaiah 54:5 (NASB) "For your husband is your Maker, whose name is the Lord of hosts; and your Redeemer is the Holy One of Israel, who is called the God of all the earth."

102 John 16:33 (NASB) "These things I have spoken to you, so that in Me you may have peace. In the world you have tribulation, but take courage; I have overcome the world."

103 Carmichael, Amy. *Candles in the dark*, Pennsylvania: CLC Publications, 2001

104 Tozer, A. W., *Living as a Christian*, Michigan: Bethany House, 2009

105 John 4:10 (NASB) "Jesus answered and said to her, 'If you knew the gift of God, and who it is who says to you, 'Give Me a drink,' you would have asked Him, and He would have given you living water.'"

106 Carmichael, Amy. *Candles in the dark*, Pennsylvania: CLC Publications, 2001

107 Psalm 27:14 (AMP) "Wait for and confidently expect the Lord; be strong and let your heart take courage; yes, wait for and confidently expect the Lord."

108 Isaiah 64:4 (NASB) "For from days of old they have not heard or perceived by ear, nor has the eye seen a God besides You, who acts in behalf of the one who waits for Him."

109 Numbers 9:20-22 (NCV) "Sometimes the cloud was over it only a few days. At the Lord's command the people camped, and at his command they moved. Sometimes the cloud stayed only from dusk until dawn; when the cloud lifted the next morning, the people moved. When the cloud lifted, day or night, the people moved. The cloud might stay over the Tent for two days, a month, or a year. As long as it stayed, the people camped, but when it lifted, they moved."

110 Deuteronomy 8:2 (NASB) "You shall remember all the way which the Lord your God has led you in the wilderness these forty years, that He might humble you, testing you, to know what was in your heart, whether you would keep His commandments or not."

111 James 1:2-4 (NIV) "Consider it pure joy, my brothers and sisters, whenever you face trials of many kinds, because you know that the testing of your faith produces perseverance. Let perseverance finish its work so that you may be mature and complete, not lacking anything."

112 Isaiah 55:8 (NKJV) "For My thoughts are not your thoughts, nor are your ways My ways, says the Lord."

113 Ecclesiastes 3:1 (NASB) "There is an appointed time for everything. And there is a time for every event under heaven."

114 Jeremiah 29:11 (NASB) "For I know the plans that I have for you,' declares the Lord, 'plans for welfare and not for calamity to give you a future and a hope."

115 Jeremiah 17:7-8 (NASB) "Blessed is the man who trusts in the Lord and whose trust is the Lord. For he will be like a tree planted by the water, that extends its roots by a stream and will not fear when the heat comes; but its leaves will be green, and it will not be anxious in a year of drought nor cease to yield fruit."

116 Cunningham, Loren, "*Daring to Live on the Edge*" W: YMAM (Youth With A Mission) Publishing, 1991

117 2 Samuel 5:23-24 (NCV) "When David prayed to the Lord, he answered, 'Don't attack the Philistines from the front. Instead, go around and attack them in front of the balsam trees. When you hear the sound of marching in the tops of the balsam trees, act quickly. I, the Lord, will have gone ahead of you to defeat the Philistine army.'"

118 Psalm 27:14 (AMP) "Wait for and confidently expect the Lord; be strong and let your heart take courage; yes, wait for and confidently expect the Lord."

119 Cowman, L. B., *Springs in the Valley*, Michigan: Zondervan, 2016

120 Chambers, Oswald. *The Place of Help*, Michigan: Oswald Chambers Publications, 1935

121 Cowman, L. B. *Streams in the Desert*, Michigan: Zondervan, 1997

122 Carrell, Rebecca. *Holy Jellybeans*, Indiana: Westbow Press, 2016

123 Matthew 14:25-33 (NLT) "About three o'clock in the morning Jesus came toward them, walking on the water. When the disciples saw him walking on the water, they were terrified. In their fear, they cried out, 'It's a ghost!' But Jesus spoke to them at once. 'Don't be afraid,' he said. 'Take courage. I am here' Then Peter called to him, 'Lord, if it's really you, tell me to come to you, walking on the water.' 'Yes, come,' Jesus said. So Peter went over the side of the boat and walked on the water toward Jesus. But when he saw the strong wind and the waves, he was terrified and began to sink. 'Save me, Lord!' he shouted. Jesus immediately reached out and grabbed him. 'You have so little faith,' Jesus said. 'Why did you doubt me?' When they climbed back into the boat, the wind stopped. Then the disciples worshiped him. 'You really are the Son of God!' they exclaimed.'"

124 Psalm 107:29 (NASB) "He caused the storm to be still, so that the waves of the sea were hushed."

125 Isaiah 25:4 (NKJV) "For You have been a strength to the poor, a strength to the needy in his distress, a refuge from the storm, a shade from the heat; for the blast of the terrible ones is as a storm against the wall."

126 Cowman, L. B. *Streams in the Desert*, Michigan: Zondervan, 1997

127 Blackaby, Henry and Richard Blackaby, Claude King, *Experiencing God*, Tennessee: B & H Publishing, 2007

128 Cowman, L. B. *Streams in the Desert*, Michigan: Zondervan, 1997

129 1 Peter 5:7 (NKJV) "casting all your care upon Him, for He cares for you."

130 Psalm 139:12 (NASB) "Even the darkness is not dark to You, and the night is as bright as the day. Darkness and light are alike to You."

131 Psalm 18:28 (NIV) "You, Lord, keep my lamp burning; my God turns my darkness into light."

132 Psalm 112:4 (NIV) "Even in darkness light dawns for the upright, for those who are gracious and compassionate and righteous."

133 John 8:12 (NASB) "Then Jesus again spoke to them, saying, 'I am the Light of the world; he who follows Me will not walk in the darkness, but will have the Light of life.'"

134 John 12:46 (NASB) "I have come as Light into the world, so that everyone who believes in Me will not remain in darkness."

135 Lamentations 3:21-24 (NASB) "This I recall to my mind, therefore I have hope, The Lord's loving kindnesses indeed never cease, for His compassions never fail. They are new every morning; great is Thy Faithfulness. The Lord is my portion, says my soul, 'Therefore I have hope in Him'"

136 Psalm 62:8 (NIV) "Trust in him at all times, O people; pour out your heart before him; God is a refuge for us. Selah."

137 Mark 4:37-39 (NKJV) "And a great windstorm arose, and the waves beat into the boat, so that it was already filling. But He was in the stern, asleep on a pillow. And they awoke Him and said to Him, 'Teacher, do You not care that we are perishing?' Then He arose and rebuked the wind, and said to the sea, 'Peace, be still!' And the wind ceased and there was a great calm."

138 Matthew 9:18-25 (NASB) "While He was saying these things to them, a synagogue official came and bowed down before Him, and said, "My daughter has just died; but come and lay Your hand on her, and she will live. ...when the crowd had been sent out, He entered and took her by the hand, and the girl got up."

139 Luke 23:33-43 (NASB) "When they came to the place called The Skull, there they crucified Him and the criminals, one on the right and the other on the left. ...One of the criminals who were hanged there was hurling abuse at Him, saying, 'Are You not the Christ? Save Yourself and us!' But the other answered, and rebuking him said, 'Do you not even fear God, since you are under the same sentence of condemnation? And we indeed are suffering justly, for we are receiving what we deserve for our deeds; but this man has done nothing wrong.' And he was saying, 'Jesus, remember me when You come in Your kingdom!' And He said to him, 'Truly I say to you, today you shall be with Me in Paradise.'"

140 Matthew 15:30-31 (NASB) "And large crowds came to Him, bringing with them those who were lame, crippled, blind, mute, and many others, and they laid them down at His feet; and He healed them. So the crowd marveled as they saw the mute speaking, the crippled restored, and the lame walking, and the blind seeing; and they glorified the God of Israel."

141 Romans 8:26-27 (NASB) "In the same way the Spirit also helps our weakness; for we do not know how to pray as we should, but the Spirit Himself intercedes for us with groanings too deep for words; and He who searches the hearts knows what the mind of the Spirit is, because He intercedes for the saints according to the will of God."

142 Philippians 4:19 (NASB) "And my God will supply all your needs according to His riches in glory in Christ Jesus."

143 Romans 8:32 (NASB) "He who did not spare His own Son, but delivered Him over for us all, how will He not also with Him freely give us all things?"

144 James 1:17 (NASB) "Every good thing given and every perfect gift is from above, coming down from the Father of lights, with whom there is no variation or shifting shadow."

145 Blackaby, Henry and Richard. *Experiencing God Day-by-Day*, Tennessee: B&H Publishing Group, 1997

146 2 Kings 6:14-17 The king of Aram, "sent horses and chariots and a great army there, and they came by night and surrounded the city. Now when the attendant of the man of God had risen early and gone out, behold, an army with horses and chariots was circling the city. And his servant said to him, 'Alas, my master! What shall we do?' So he answered, 'Do not fear, for those who are with us are more than those who are with them.' Then Elisha prayed and said, 'O Lord, I pray, open his eyes that he may see.' And the Lord opened the servant's eyes and he saw; and behold, the mountain was full of horses and chariots of fire all around Elisha."

147 2 Corinthians 4:18 (NIV) "So we fix our eyes not on what is seen, but on what is unseen. For what is seen is temporary, but what is unseen is eternal."

148 Luke 10:38-42 (NASB) "Now as they were traveling along, He entered a village; and a woman named Martha welcomed Him into her home. She had a sister called Mary, who was seated at the Lord's feet, listening to His word. But Martha was distracted with

all her preparations; and she came up to Him and said, 'Lord, do You not care that my sister has left me to do all the serving alone? Then tell her to help me.' But the Lord answered and said to her, 'Martha, Martha, you are worried and bothered about so many things; but only one thing is necessary, for Mary has chosen the good part, which shall not be taken away from her.'"

149 Micah 6:8 (NLT) "...the Lord has told you what is good, and this is what he requires of you: to do what is right, to love mercy, and to walk humbly with your God."

150 Mark 12:30-31 (NLT) Jesus said, "And you must love the Lord your God with all your heart, all your soul, all your mind, and all your strength. The second is equally important: Love your neighbor as yourself. No other commandment is greater than these."

151 Exodus 36:1 (NASB) "...The Lord has given them wisdom and understanding to know how to do all the work..."

152 Matthew 17:20 (NKJV) Jesus said to them, "... I say to you, if you have faith as a mustard seed, you will say to this mountain, 'Move from here to there,' and it will move; and nothing will be impossible for you."

153 Ephesians 3:20 (AMP) "Now to Him who is able to [carry out His purpose and] do superabundantly more than all that we dare ask or think [infinitely beyond our greatest prayers, hopes, or dreams], according to His power that is at work within us"

154 2 Timothy 3:16-17 (NASB) "all Scripture is inspired by God and profitable for teaching, for reproof, for correction, for training in righteousness; so that the man of God may be adequate, equipped for every good work."

155 Philippians 2:13 (NASB) "it is God who is at work in you, both to will and to work for His good pleasure."

156 2 Corinthians 9:8 (NKJV) "And God is able to make all grace abound toward you, that you, always having all sufficiency in all things, may have an abundance for every good work."

157 Psalm 73:25-26 (NIV) "Whom have I in heaven but you? And earth has nothing I desire besides you. My flesh and my heart may fail, but God is the strength of my heart and my portion forever."

158 Ephesians 6:10 (AMP) "Be strong in the Lord [draw your strength from Him and be empowered through your union with Him] and in the power of His [boundless] might."

159 John 15:5 (NASB) "I am the vine, you are the branches; he who abides in Me and I in him, he bears much fruit, for apart from Me you can do nothing."

160 2 Chronicles 20:22 (NIV) "As they began to sing and praise, the LORD set ambushes against the men of Ammon and Moab and Mount Seir who were invading Judah, and they were defeated."

161 Duewel, Wesley L., *Touch the World through Prayer*, Michigan: Zondervan, 1986

162 Duewel, Wesley L., *Touch the World through Prayer*, Michigan: Zondervan, 1986

163 Jeremiah 32:17 (NIV) "Ah, Sovereign LORD, you have made the heavens and the earth by your great power and outstretched arm. Nothing is too hard for you."

164 Ephesians 6:18 (NLT) "Pray in the Spirit at all times and on every occasion. Stay alert and be persistent in your prayers for all believers everywhere."

165 Acts 12:5-16 (NASB) "Peter was kept in the prison, but prayer for him was being made fervently by the church to God. ...Peter was sleeping between two soldiers, bound with two chains, and guards in front of the door were watching over the prison. ...an angel of the Lord suddenly appeared and a light shone in the cell; and he struck Peter's side and woke him up, saying, 'Get up quickly.' And his chains fell off his hands. The angel led him out, and when they had passed the first and second guard, they came to the iron gate that leads into the city, which opened for them by itself ...."

166 Matthew 13:58 (NKJV) "Now He did not do many mighty works there because of their unbelief."

167 Luke 9:23 (NKJV) "Then He said to them all, 'If anyone desires to come after Me, let him deny himself, and take up his cross daily, and follow Me."

168 Caine, Christine. *Unstoppable*, Michigan: Zondervan, 2014

169 1 Corinthians 1:27-28 (NLT) God chose things the world considers foolish in order to shame those who think they are wise. And he chose things that are powerless to shame those who are powerful. God chose things despised by the world, things counted as nothing at all, and used them to bring to nothing what the world considers important.
170 Platt, David. *Follow Me*, Tennessee: LifeWay Press, 2013

171 1 Corinthians 9:24-25 (NET Bible) "Do you not know that all the runners in a stadium compete, but only one receives the prize? So run to win. Each competitor must exercise self-control in everything. They do it to receive a perishable crown, but we an imperishable one."

172 Philippians 3:12-14 (NKJV) "Not that I have already attained, or am already perfected; but I press on, that I may lay hold of that for which Christ Jesus has also laid hold of me. Brethren, I do not count myself to have apprehended; but one thing I do, forgetting those things which are behind and reaching forward to those things which are ahead, I press toward the goal for the prize of the upward call of God in Christ Jesus."

173 Philippians 1:6 (NKJV) "being confident of this very thing, that He who has begun a good work in you will complete it until the day of Jesus Christ."

174 Hebrews 12:1-2 (NKJV) "Therefore we also, since we are surrounded by so great a cloud of witnesses, let us lay aside every weight, and the sin which so easily ensnares us, and let us run with endurance the race that is set before us, looking unto Jesus, the author and finisher of our faith, who for the joy that was set before Him endured the cross, despising the shame, and has sat down at the right hand of the throne of God."

Thank you for reading.

The Forgotten Resting Place

Lisa Buffaloe

www.ingramcontent.com/pod-product-compliance
Lightning Source LLC
Chambersburg PA
CBHW081506040426
42446CB00017B/3413